Spiritual Traces

Spiritual Traces

*Reflections and Conversations
on Contemporary Art*

AARON ROSEN

CASCADE *Books* · Eugene, Oregon

SPIRITUAL TRACES
Reflections and Conversations on Contemporary Art

Cascade Books
An Imprint of Wipf and Stock Publishers
199 W. 8th Ave., Suite 3
Eugene, OR 97401

www.wipfandstock.com

PAPERBACK ISBN: 979-8-3852-3540-7
HARDCOVER ISBN: 979-8-3852-3541-4
EBOOK ISBN: 979-8-3852-3542-1

Cataloguing-in-Publication data:

Names: Rosen, Aaron, author.

Title: Spiritual traces : reflections and conversations on contemporary art / Aaron Rosen.

Description: Eugene, OR: Cascade Books, 2025 | Includes bibliographical references.

Identifiers: ISBN 979-8-3852-3540-7 (paperback) | ISBN 979-8-3852-3541-4 (hardcover) | ISBN 979-8-3852-3542-1 (ebook)

Subjects: LCSH: Art and religion. | Art, Contemporary—21st century. | Art, Modern—themes, motives.

Classification: N7790 R67 2025 (print) | N7790 (ebook)

To Michael Takeo Magruder
Devoted Artist and Friend

Contents

PART II. CONVERSATIONS

List of Figures

Acknowledgments

THIS BOOK IS DEDICATED to a dear artist friend as well as godfather to my son Arthur, Michael Takeo Magruder. Michael belongs to a group of artists who profoundly shaped my development as a curator and thinker about contemporary art during my years in London. By the time I met Michael—as well as artists Güler Ates, G. Roland Biermann, and Leni Dothan, who also became close friends—I had already trained as an academic and was ensconced in my first permanent academic post at King's College London. And yet in many ways it was not until I started working closely with artists on creative projects that I recognized how little I really knew about how artists think and work through dilemmas.

While working with Michael and others, I realized the extent to which technical challenges can simultaneously constitute philosophical quandaries. Not unlike the way rabbis in the Talmud debate seemingly mundane matters only to end up formulating important theological distinctions. For all intents and purposes, I found my footing as a curator by apprenticing myself to artists, letting them teach me not only how to curate their work but how to ask them the right kinds of questions, the ones that jar loose new insights and revelations. The essays and conversations in this book channel those lessons, which I am still learning from those artists and many others. This book would have been impossible not only without the artists who appear in these pages, but the ones who first trained my eyes and hands.

I also want to thank two mentors who passed away in recent years, each of whom knew intuitively how to look with artists' eyes. The first is my beloved doctoral supervisor at Cambridge, Graham Howes. Graham was a collector in every sense. The walls of the home he shared with his wife, Shirley, were festooned with books and art, the ornaments of a life rich in adventures great and small, geographic and intellectual. In a sense, Graham taught me what it meant to be a curator of one's own life, from the books one read to the friends one drew close. Graham reveled in the company of clever people, and while that might sound elitist, it was in fact the opposite. Despite spending nearly his entire student and professional life at Cambridge, Graham was prepared—indeed thrilled—to see gifts in people of truly any background or identity. And he was profoundly committed to offering assistance, especially when he felt someone was unappreciated, whether by others or themselves. For my part, Graham offered the perfect blend of paternal propping-up and light-hearted encouragement. As I labored under obscenely self-important struggles with my thesis, Graham reminded me frequently that the PhD was, in the end, "just a vocational degree."

After leaving Cambridge, I served as a post-doctoral fellow at Yale, where the retired priest Ralph Peterson tracked me down based on shared interests in religion and modern art. Incurably optimistic, Ralph had an unabashed belief in the power of the arts—enough to make many Protestants blush! Countless times, I remember him earnestly paraphrasing Dostoevsky: beauty will save the world. Beauty for Ralph was no mere indulgence, it was serious stuff and among the most enduring things communities can achieve together. It is fitting then that the crown jewel of Ralph's professional life was commissioning the serene Louise Nevelson Chapel for St. Peter's Lutheran Church in New York City. We rightly give a lot of credit to artists, especially an artist as great as Nevelson, but visionary patrons are their own rare creative species. Ralph knew this innately, and proudly retold what he considered Nevelson's greatest compliment to him, "Ralph, you old fucker, you're an artist like the rest of us." Only a special kind of priest could see this for what it was: a benediction. In a similar spirit, I have come to see myself, if not as an artist, as at least a fellow traveler. This book is an invitation to join those travels.

Introduction

A HALF DOZEN YEARS ago, when I began most of the essays and interviews in this book, I would not have dreamed of calling it *Spiritual Traces*. During my years in Cambridge, I remember a senior academic dismissing talk of spirituality as "all a bit Californian." In other words, spuriously new age, unworthy of serious study. This insouciant remark, and the presumptions behind it, stuck with me longer than I care to admit.

In retrospect, I imbibed too readily the notion that spirituality was merely a convenient label for diffuse feelings about religion. It has certainly become trendy, even reflexive in some communities, for people to declare themselves "spiritual but not religious." And sometimes this does obscure more than illuminate the reasons why an individual rejects a specific faith or casts off a congregation or community of origin. But designating oneself "spiritual" can do much more than name a negative, and I underrated this in some of my earlier writings on art and religion.

Spirituality can of course mean myriad things to different individuals and communities. And it remains notoriously difficult to define, whether at the individual or social level. One of the first issues is that the oft-invoked dichotomy between spirituality and religion rarely holds up in everyday life. In fact, recent surveys have shown that the people most likely to define themselves as spiritual are those who identify as religious, confounding easy binaries.[1] It might seem easier to focus solely on those who explicitly disavow religious affiliation. Indeed, a great deal of attention in recent years has focused on the rise of religious "Nones" in the United States: individuals who answer "none" when asked by researchers to name the religious group to which they belong or with whom they identify. This group has ballooned dramatically in the twenty-first century—for reasons we are just beginning to understand—to the extent that Nones are "now the same size

1. Ammerman, *Sacred Stories, Spiritual Tribes*, 4.

xvii

as both Roman Catholics and evangelical Protestants," the two largest religious groups in the US.[2] Yet even this stunning statistic is just as liable to confuse as clarify, since these Nones are hardly a monolithic group and can run the gamut from committed atheists to lifelong spiritual seekers. Moreover, spiritual Nones rarely live separate lives from "Somes"—Elizabeth Drescher's egalitarian term for the religiously affiliated—with whom they exist in "frequent spiritual proximity."[3]

In the end, rather than vainly seeking to pinpoint the perimeters of spirituality writ large—or worse yet, impose them—we are better off listening closely to the "spiritual stories" that people tell about their lives, letting narratives rather than theoretical constructs guide our inquiries.[4] Sometimes, studying a sufficient number of these stories will enable scholars to sketch wider trends. Yet even when that proves challenging, and broader features remain elusive to theological and sociological analysis, the endeavor is hardly less interesting, or less important. This book offers an exercise in listening, anchored by the belief that some of the most compelling spiritual stories being told today are those of visual artists, both through their art itself and the way they describe their process of art-making. For all their diversity, one thing we can say about the finest artists—of all stripes—is that they are devoted to deep self-reflection. So when they describe themselves or their art practice as spiritually engaged, our ears should prick up.

I set off to discover "spiritual traces" because I was interested in those places where spirituality feels latent, ephemeral, or on the edge of possibility. In other words: anything but stable and obvious. It was important to me to write about and interview artists whose approach to spirituality needed to be teased out, where a certain amount of sleuthing was required and rewarded. While I would hardly claim to be the first to do so, it is astonishing how seldom this kind of groundwork has been done. In the vast corpus of contemporary artist interviews, for example, it is relatively rare to hear interviewers press their subjects on spiritual matters, even when artists leave the door tantalizingly ajar.

There are even fewer books devoted to exploring spiritual questions with contemporary visual artists. One exception is the work of the sociologist Robert Wuthnow, who interviewed dozens of practitioners for *Creative Spirituality: The Way of the Artist.* While the range of Wuthnow's

2. Burge, *Nones*, 2.

3. Drescher, *Choosing Our Religion*, 9.

4. Ammerman, *Sacred Stories, Spiritual Tribes*, 14.

conversations is impressive, his decision to cover "the artist" in a broad sense—from poets to musicians to visual artists—offers little opportunity to learn what sensory strategies, source material, or influences might be common to visual artists. For the most part, actual works of art fade to the background as Wuthnow dwells on artists' accounts of what it means to be an artist. Ironically, this ignores a key piece of the puzzle, for to be a visual artist, in particular, is to wager on the capacity of things and images to accomplish the work of meaning for—and indeed beyond—them.

An indisputable champion of creatives, Wuthnow appears caught between defensive and offensive imperatives. On the one hand, he wants to shield artists from marginalization as mere "spiritual dabblers,"[5] while on the other hand he speculates that artists might "increasingly become the spiritual leaders of our time."[6] A quarter-century onward, amidst a wider spiritual turn, Wuthnow's defenses feel less urgent. Meanwhile, as a flurry of self-appointed spiritual gurus and other lifestyle influencers flood social media, it seems like wishful thinking to hope that serious artists might rise to the role of society's "spiritual leaders."

So what can we say about visual artists today and the spiritual trajectories they pursue in their work? One feature that emerged frequently in my interviews and discussions with artists is the increasing number who noted the importance of ritual in their spiritual and creative lives. A significant catalyst appears to have been the COVID-19 pandemic. Amidst monotonous stretches of quarantine, my family and I certainly found that the demarcation of sacred time offered by ritual—in our case the weekly observance of Shabbat and Jewish holidays—quieted our minds and introduced a spirit of anticipation.

As later research and reporting has shown, my family was hardly alone in turning to spiritual traditions for a sense of structured, sacred time in this strange period. Meanwhile, spurred in part by the Black Lives Matter movement, discourses around self-care and rest as tactics of replenishment, resilience, and resistance for minority communities has offered complementary ways to think about sacred time. In my discussions with artists, both the desire to initiate sacred time and attend to self-care appeared often as motivations for observing ritual, sometimes in tandem, as Sobia Ahmad describes.

5. Wuthnow, *Creative Spirituality,* 10.
6. Wuthnow, *Creative Spirituality,* 266.

Several artists told me that meditation was a regular part of their studio life, including Bernd Haussmann, who teaches workshops on mindfulness, intertwined with creative practice. Other activities mentioned by artists included offering prayers or taking a contemplative walk before commencing work, lighting candles or incense in the studio, or using music to set a spiritual metronome for themselves. Indeed, I found the discussion of ritual cropping up in conversations enough that over time I began to ask artists directly if there was a ritual that they used to focus their creative energies. Interestingly, in some cases artists began by saying no, as Barbara Takenaga did, but in the process of describing their practice they realized that they did in fact incorporate ritual in their practice—they simply had not framed it to themselves in that way previously.

A number of the artists I feature in this book reference specific religious rituals. Alyssa Sakina Mumtaz created a series of paintings of Muslim prayer beads that she uses daily, which she envisions as "simultaneously a love letter to the many other religious traditions that utilize beads as a support for prayer." MyLoan Dinh has also found herself creating works with prayer beads, including malas used in Buddhist and Hindu prayer and meditation. Anne Mourier began her career creating works that honored the daily, unheralded rituals often performed by women in the home. Over time, she has increasingly sought to involve her audiences in the performance of ritual, drawing inspiration from humble acts of devotion and fellowship, such as Mary perfuming the feet of Jesus (John 12:3). Ezra Bookman, meanwhile, utilized the lessons he learned from curating ritual experiences at the "God-optional" Jewish community of Lab/Shul in New York to found Ritualist, which he describes as "the first ever creative studio specializing in the design of secular rituals."

Most of the interviews in this book initially appeared in *Image Journal,* a quarterly magazine dedicated to "art, mystery, and faith." It has been an honor over the past half dozen years to serve as the visual art editor for *Image,* working with James K. A. Smith, Mary Kenagy Mitchell, and a host of other talented editors. *Image's* reputation for thoughtful explorations of spirituality and the arts means that some artists have found me through the journal, while others have opened up about spiritual connections in ways they might not have shared with other communities of readers. The gestalt of *Image,* which favors slow, deliberate forms of creation and contemplation, also means that I have adapted my interview style since *Brushes with Faith*, my previous volume of collected essays and interviews.[7] Rather than beginning with audio recordings, I now favor informal, unrecorded conversations with artists, followed by the rather old-fashioned form of epistolary interviews (the fact that by epistolary I mean email exchanges makes me a generational relic in another sense!). The insightful responses by artists in these interviews reflects their ability to take a deep breath and compose their thoughts. What is lost in spontaneity—not many inadvertent admissions or Freudian slips to be found here, I am afraid—is gained in sustained, deliberate reflection.

Like *Brushes with Faith*, this volume is divided evenly between essays—primarily commissioned for exhibition catalogues—and interviews. I see the division as a formal and heuristic one. In reality, this entire book is rooted in my relationships and conversations with artists, whether the result in a given instance was an essay or an interview. As I wrote in my previous book, I hope that "what I lack in distance, I make up for with the kind of details and disclosures that can only be conjured through intimacy and reciprocity."[8] If anything, this closeness has only deepened in recent years, as I have grown into my vocation as a curator, alongside—and often interwoven with—my roles as a scholar and writer.

Some of my first forays as a curator occurred when I founded the Stations of the Cross public art project, curating iterations in London, Washington, DC, and New York City, which I reflect upon in one of the essays in this volume. However, my greatest growth as a curator has occurred over the past several years, since founding the non-profit Parsonage Gallery in coastal Maine. When I decided to move back to my home state with my son Arthur, to the former shipbuilding town of Searsport, I had the good fortune to stumble across a historic estate, much in need of restoration yet clearly destined to be a gallery. It was built in 1831 as a parsonage for an important abolitionist minister, Stephen Thurston, and his wife, Clara Thurston (née Benson). When I started looking at the local archives, I discovered that Clara was Winslow Homer's aunt. Winslow and his mother Henrietta Benson Homer—a gifted watercolorist who taught him the form—stayed at the parsonage and Winslow even produced some of his juvenilia here.[9] With this artistic and religious lineage, the space seemed perfect for a gallery exploring the intersection of spirituality, ecology, and creativity.

7. Rosen, *Brushes with Faith*.
8. Rosen, *Brushes with Faith*, xix.
9. Cross, *Winslow Homer*, 5.

In a modest way, the Parsonage has become a beacon for artists attracted to these themes, both within New England and beyond. Many of the conversations recorded in the pages of this book evolved organically into exhibitions at the gallery, embellishing the spiritual traces first sketched out in conversations. To me, this signifies a sense of promise not only for my own experiment here in Penobscot Bay but other artistic endeavors in venues outside metropolitan centers. The overstory of the art world gets a lot of attention, but as the twenty-first century progresses, I suspect that the most exciting and sustainable growth is likely to happen at the ground level, nourished by engaged communities. And what is fruitful for art may prove equally so for spirituality.

PART I.
REFLECTIONS

FIGURE 1.1

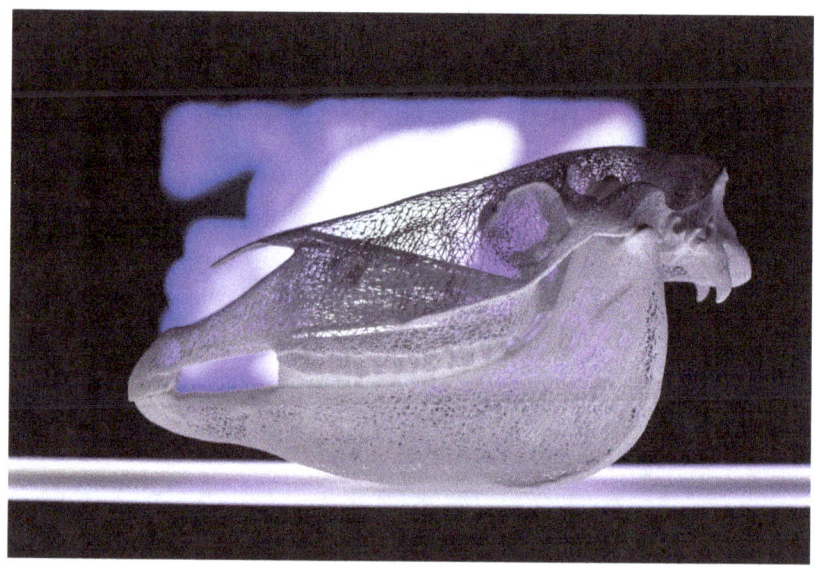

Reinventing Tradition

1. The Bible and Contemporary Art in America

WRITING IN 1983, THE esteemed theologian John W. Dixon Jr. set some parameters for his inquiry into biblical art:

> The problem of "The Bible in American Art" must be distinguished carefully from the larger problem of "religion in American art." They are not the same thing nor is the smaller question rightly understood as a special case of the larger; they are in some degree different problems, however much the areas overlap.[1]

While visual art—and the way we study it—has changed dramatically in the intervening decades, Dixon's intuition remains helpful. In previous publications, including my survey *Art and Religion in the 21st Century*, I have cast a wider net, considering the numerous ways in which religious themes and questions surface in contemporary art.[2] In the present essay, I want to focus specifically on some of the ways in which the Bible appears in recent American art, and what new challenges and possibilities arise.

Within the guideposts suggested by Dixon, the terrain looks dramatically different forty years later. To begin with, the question of what should

---

1. Dixon Jr., "Bible in American Painting," 157. The present essay was commissioned for an updated edition of that project. It appeared as "The Bible in American Visual Art," in *The Bible in America*, edited by Claudia Setzer and David Shefferman, and I am grateful to the publisher and the editors for permission to reprint it here.

2. Rosen, *Art and Religion in the 21st Century*. Small portions of that volume—namely on the artists Andres Serrano and Michael Takeo Magruder—have been adapted for the present essay, with permission from the publisher.

count as art is highly tendentious. Though Dixon was writing at a time of burgeoning experimentation in fields such as performance, installation, and video art, his essay focuses on painting. While artists in this period were contesting and dismantling traditional boundaries, academics often struggled to catch up. This was doubly true of religious scholars, whose definitions of art tended to lag behind the evolving categories of art historians and critics. Dixon, for example, concludes his essay with an extensive discussion of Abstract Expressionism, casting it as the apotheosis of modern art.

While this would have delighted Mark Rothko, who famously predicted a thousand-year reign for abstraction in the visual arts,[3] the truth is that even then a generation of younger artists was already scrambling to dethrone the orthodoxy he promulgated. An updated assessment of the place of the Bible in American art must attempt to do justice to the multifarious practice of contemporary artists. With this in mind, I will give an indication of this variety by analyzing examples from three fields that have seen tremendous growth in recent decades: graphic novels, new media (e.g., digital art), and environmental art.

Art is not the only thorny term in the search for "the Bible in American Art." Even "American" is less self-evident than it might first appear. Dixon seeks to identify an authentically American spirit in the visual arts, capable of standing alongside what he views as the more coherent categories of, say, French or Chinese art. It is no mistake that he concludes his survey with a paean to the Abstract Expressionists, who—despite the inspiration they drew from various sources, including European Surrealists— believed they had pioneered the first truly American school of painting; a claim trumpeted by the critic Clement Greenberg, who termed these works "American-Type Painting."[4]

While subsequent generations of American artists have continued to play a leading role in the art world, it is increasingly difficult to make claims for any dominant or distinctly American school or style of art. The art world might have epicenters in New York and Los Angeles, but it is now indisputably global, with major art schools, museums, biennials, and fairs from London to Berlin, São Paolo, and Dubai. In this global context, the most important dialogues between artists, curators, dealers, critics, and academics are less nationally determined than ever. "American art" is a

3. Breslin, *Mark Rothko*, 431.
4. Greenberg, *Art and Culture*, 208.

useful descriptor to frame broad inquiries, or to discuss artistic responses to specific issues, such as the terrorist attacks of September 11 or police violence towards African Americans. But in many cases it can be either too small or too big a category to do much conceptual work. When it comes to assessing the role of the Bible in contemporary American art, we must be cognizant, on the one hand, of the way in which artists today continually look outwards, beyond their country of origin. At the same time, we must pay attention to artists' hybrid identities, considering how their religious, ethnic, gender, and sexual self-definitions shape their sense of what it means to be an American.

There is one more important piece of the puzzle missing from Dixon's analysis: context. Dixon offers sensitive reflections on key works, especially by Thomas Eakins, Albert Pinkham Ryder, and Barnett Newman, and he is well aware of how individual spectators might devise different interpretations of such works. However, like many scholars of his era, he pays hardly any attention to the material conditions in which such encounters occur. One of the most promising developments of twenty-first-century scholarship has been a widening of scholars' fields of vision to encompass varied dimensions of visual and material experience, and the discourses that shape and structure these encounters. One of the key figures in this material turn is David Morgan, who helpfully coins the term "sacred gaze" to describe how images *become* religious in our eyes. He writes:

> *Sacred gaze* is a term that designates the particular configuration of ideas, attitudes, and customs that informs a religious act of seeing as it occurs within a given cultural and historical setting. A sacred gaze is the manner in which a way of seeing invests an image, a viewer, or an act of viewing with spiritual significance. The study of religious visual culture is therefore the study of images, but also the practices and habits that rely on images as well as the attitudes and preconceptions that inform vision as a cultural act.[5]

As Morgan's analysis makes clear, categorizing a subject as biblical is not only conditioned by multiple material, cultural, and ideological factors, but the designation itself structures and conditions religious possibilities. With this in mind, I will offer some reflections about how biblical references are activated differently within disparate spaces, from religious institutions to museums. In brief, then, this essay will revolve around three basic questions about contemporary American art: *Who* engages with biblical

5. Morgan, *Sacred Gaze*, 3.

subjects? *What* methods and media do they use? And *where, when,* and *how* are biblical references rendered visible?

PIETY AND IMPROPRIETY

The mere mention of a contemporary artist engaging with biblical subject matter summons competing stereotypes. On the one hand stands the artist as purveyor of pious kitsch; on the other, the talented but godless iconoclast. Both stereotypes are problematic in their own right, and it is important to clear away some of the presumptions they entail. Taking the former stereotype first, we might turn our attention to Thomas Kinkade, the artist behind such ubiquitous works as *The Cross* (2010), which depicts Calvary glistening amidst candy-floss-colored clouds. While such works may well be considered kitsch, this makes them no less interesting when it comes to assessing the place of the Bible in American culture.

As many as one in twenty American homes owns a print or other object produced by Kinkade, the self-anointed "painter of light."[6] Kinkade might lack the brooding Romanticism of Caspar David Friedrich, but for many contemporary Americans, his insertion of Christian symbols into a proudly sweeping vista appears to be no less religiously charged than the works of his German precursor. Similarly, Jon McNaughton's *One Nation under God* (2009)—in which Jesus clasps the US Constitution, surrounded by the founding fathers—might rankle contemporary critics with its strongly didactic content. However, it sits within a tradition of Last Judgment paintings that have referenced the perceived heroes and villains of their own day.[7]

Kinkade and McNaughton muster historically effective strategies from the art of the past to convey an image of the United States as it should be, whether conjuring images of a halcyon, biblically anchored past, or preparing for an apocalyptically tinged struggle to "make America great again."[8] As Morgan notes, "simply scorning [such works] misses the opportunity

---

6. Boylan, "Introduction," 1.

7. Morgan, "Art of Jon McNaughton."

8. McNaughton sells reproductions of drawings of Donald Trump paired with quotes that "will make you think, laugh, and cheer." See http://jonmcnaughton.com/trump-drawings-and-quotes-1/.

to understand something powerful moving through many religious sub-cultures in the United States today."[9]

On the opposite side of the spectrum stands the image of artists as cynical unbelievers, scorning the Bible to the cackling applause of intellectuals. A string of well-publicized controversies from the mid-eighties to the present have tended to reinforce a predictable pattern. Various artists have found themselves at the center of conflagrations over biblical imagery, including Renee Cox, Chris Ofili, and Cosimo Cavallaro. But the reception of two works from the late eighties demonstrates this trend particularly well: Andres Serrano's photograph *Piss Christ* (1987) and David Wojnarowicz's unfinished short film, *A Fire in My Belly* (1986–1987). *Piss Christ*—which shows a crucifix suspended in urine—first came to national attention when US Senator Jesse Helms used an exhibition of it in 1989 as a pretext to call for severe funding cuts to the National Endowment for the Arts; part of a larger assault on what the senator considered the propagation of anti-Christian values.

When the work was exhibited in New York in 2012, Republican lawmakers, the Catholic League, and conservative pundits demanded unsuccessfully that President Barack Obama denounce the work, repeating the same charges of blasphemy that had been leveled against the piece a generation earlier. For its part, Wojnarowicz's video exploring suffering and myth became a lightning rod for controversy during the 2010–11 exhibition *Hide/Seek: Difference and Desire in American Portraiture* at the Smithsonian's National Portrait Gallery. Labeled anti-Christian "hate speech" by the Catholic League and key Republican congressmen who threatened to withhold federal funding for the Smithsonian, the work was pulled from the exhibition.[10]

These recent controversies expose what could almost be termed nostalgia for the culture wars of a bygone era; those good old days when threatening public funding for the arts and bemoaning assaults on "traditional values" felt fresh and invigorating! Digging beneath the surface, these recycled jeremiads have very little to do with either protecting the Bible or Christianity. As confrontational as its title may sound, *Piss Christ* can be read more coherently as a devotional image, produced by an artist born and bred in a Brooklyn neighborhood steeped in Catholicism. What better way to meditate on the torments and degradation of Christ—both in his time

---

9. Morgan, "Art of Jon McNaughton."

10. "Arts," *Catholic League*; cf. Knight, "Gay Art."

and ours—than to see his form submerged in urine? At the same time, the resplendence of the image, suffused in golden light like a Byzantine icon, also seems to signal Christ's capacity to triumph over ignominy.

Likewise, the controversy over a mere three-second section in Wojnarowicz's thirteen-minute video—in which ants crawl over a crucifix—ignores ample art historical precedents for a flayed and even putrefying Savior. We need only think of Jesus' gangrenous, weeping wounds in Matthias Grünewald's *Isenheim Altarpiece* (1515) to make a case for Wojnarowicz's *restraint* while confronting a world ravaged by HIV/AIDS, the disease which would later take his life. Ironically, reproaches of Serrano and Wojnarowicz—much like denigrations of Kinkade and McNaughton—fail to contextualize these works within the wider tradition of Christian art and spirituality. Disputes over *how* the Bible is depicted often turn out to be fights about *who* is doing the depicting.

MEDIUM AND MESSAGE

In recent decades, art has become increasingly difficult to pigeonhole into traditional categories such as painting, sculpture, printmaking, and photography. Not only do artists specialize in fields ranging from performance to video to installation art, but many have refused to define themselves by a single medium, preferring to move fluidly between different modes of expression. Rather than attempt a comprehensive overview of how the Bible has surfaced in various art forms, I want to focus instead on a few select media—namely graphic novels, digital, and environmental art—which signal the sheer breadth of recent work engaging biblical subjects. These new works do more than simply illustrate or represent the Bible. They change how we read it, disclosing tantalizing horizons for future artists.

Comics may seem at first like an unlikely, irreverent, even offensive medium through which to explore Holy Scripture. And yet, since the sixties the medium of comics has increasingly evolved, tackling serious themes while developing complex representational and narrative strategies. To many practitioners, critics, and readers, the term "comix" is preferable to comics, denoting the art form's underground roots and its complicated blend (or co-mixing) of image and text. The media theorist and graphic novelist Douglas Rushkoff is not merely puckish when he suggests that the "Bible may have actually been better off as a comic book."[11] Comix present

11. Rushkoff and Sharp, *Testament.*

the opportunity to draw out dimensions of the text that other art forms struggle to capture. R. Crumb uses his signature smutty style to disclose the bodily, even crude dimensions of the original text of Genesis, to which most translations apply a fig leaf.[12] But comix can do more than sensitize us to salacious subtexts. Through their highly adaptable structure they can also suggest new hermeneutic possibilities. In *Megillat Esther*, J. T. Waldman draws upon the haptic experience of reading the Scroll of Esther to create a work in which words and images unfurl across the page.[13]

In the comic book *Testament: Akedah*, Douglas Rushkoff and illustrator Liam Sharp interweave the story of the binding of Isaac (Gen 22) with a dystopian narrative set in the near future and mythic tales from ancient cultures.[14] The result emphasizes the palimpsistic nature of the Bible itself, composed of different authorial and editorial layers, each pointing toward different interpretive possibilities. For Rushkoff, comics is better positioned than any other medium to reveal and extend the process of the text's creation, which he compares to "open source" collaboration in computer programming.[15] While rewriting and re-imaging the Bible in this way might discomfit literalists, the intrinsically democratic spirit of such an endeavor might feel quintessentially American to others.[16]

Digital technology not only provides a powerful metaphor for understanding interpretive possibilities, it is already a key part of how many people engage with the Bible today. Bespoke software allows new methods of searching texts, comparing translations, and accessing commentaries; apps can deliver daily devotions, converting phones into Books of Hours; and social media spawns new communities of interpreters. While a number of artists have touched upon such intersections between digital technology and the Bible, no one has probed this interface in greater depth than the American artist Michael Takeo Magruder. Magruder takes Rushkoff's parallel between computer coding and biblical composition a step further, recognizing the theological implications of the coder *qua* creator. In *Visions of Our Communal Dreams v2.0* (2012), Magruder provides an apparatus for gallery visitors to help shape a shared, virtual Eden. "I sought to adopt

12. Crumb, *Genesis.*

13. Waldman, *Megillat Esther.*

14. Rushkoff, *Testament,* unpaginated.

15. Rushkoff, *Testament,* unpaginated.

16. A number of other recent graphic novels by American artists have explored biblical themes, including: Thompson, *Blankets*; Thompson, *Habibi*; Ross, *Marked*; and Panter, *Songy of Paradise.*

God's position as creator and instigator by constructing a beautiful realm of open possibilities that others could inhabit as they desired," he explains.[17]

Magruder imagines "the world's first rays of virtual sunlight illuminat[ing] a newly rendered synthetic landscape made from data and code—the fundamental building blocks of creation in the Information Age."[18] Rather than retreating from reality, this simulation models a process of collaborative world-building that can be downloaded, so to speak, into the real world. Of course, just as easily, the same technology can also generate communal nightmares, as Magruder explores in his 2014 exhibition *De/coding the Apocalypse* (Figure 1.1), which grew out of close readings of the book of Revelation. Ultimately, Magruder leaves it open to interpretation whether our ever-evolving technology—he is currently exploring the possibilities of Artificial Intelligence in his practice—will help us realize prophetic possibilities, or force open the seals of our destruction.

Our potential for self-destruction is nowhere more evident than in the rapidly accelerating effects of human-made climate change. In the United States, the political debate over climate change has been increasingly framed in terms of faith, with a sizeable number of evangelical Christians denying or expressing strong doubts about global warming in the face of overwhelming scientific evidence. At the root of this reluctance seems to be a general anxiety about scientific discourse—especially its ability to challenge biblical accounts of creation—as well as a reflexive rejection of causes associated with the political left, seen as opponents of "traditional" values.

The irony is that refusing to acknowledge this human-made catastrophe actually runs counter to a key point of Scripture, which emphasizes human responsibility for the environment. In the garden of Eden, for instance, humanity is entrusted with the stewardship of nature (Gen 1:28–30), while Noah is charged with preserving the planet's biodiversity (Gen 6:19–7:3). Building on such examples, there is a tremendous opportunity—as an increasing number of American artists have recognized—to reclaim environmental concern as a religious imperative.

One of the most innovative artists addressing this topic at the moment is Sam Van Aken. For his living sculpture, *Tree of 40 Fruits* (2008–13), he spent years painstakingly grafting branches of assorted stone fruits—including plums, apricots, peaches, and nectarines—onto a single trunk, so that all these different species might blossom and fructify together (Figure

---

17. Personal Communication with Michael Takeo Magruder, May 14, 2014.

18. Personal Communication with Michael Takeo Magruder, May 14, 2014.

1.2). As he notes, the number forty is frequently used in the Bible to symbolize a boundless multitude.[19] In this case, the number evokes the story of the flood, which according to Genesis lasted forty days and forty nights (Gen 7:4). When the floodwaters receded, and Noah finally set foot on dry land, the Bible informs us that he immediately did two things: he offered thanksgiving to the Lord (Gen 8:20) and planted a vineyard (Gen 9:20).

This second act was just as important as the first. It confirmed that Noah not only feared the Lord but believed God's promise never again to destroy the earth. Today, it is we who must promise that "As long as the earth endures, seedtime and harvest, cold and heat, summer and winter, day and night, shall not cease" (Gen 8:22). But while our roles may be reversed, we can still seal this covenant with the same simple act of faith: planting fruit. In an age of environmental catastrophe, Van Aken's *Tree of 40 Fruits* provides a hopeful symbol of blessing and abundance. For the great American landscape painters of the nineteenth century, the land that stretched before them was imbued with biblical majesty. Today, that promise must be carefully regrown, and artists amongst others must sow the seeds.

FIGURE 1.2

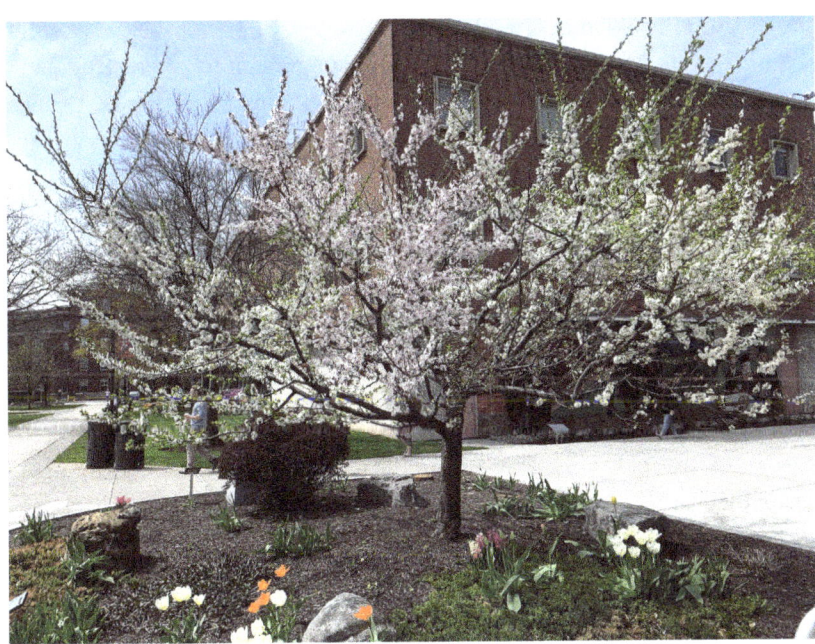

19. Lauren Salkeld interviewing Sam Van Aken, alongside *The Tree of 40 Fruit.*

PLACES AND SPACES

After considering the motivations and materials of contemporary artists, it is time to look at questions of context a bit more closely. Where is it today that we might expect to find art that deals with the Bible? The most straightforward answer, of course, is religious institutions. While religious patronage is certainly not like it was in centuries past, when it provided the main source of employment for Western artists, many American churches today have robust programs of visual art. To name just a few in New York City, we might think of the Cathedral of St. John the Divine, Trinity Church Wall Street, and St. Peter's Lutheran Church, which each have a reputation for innovative permanent installations and temporary exhibitions.

The art displayed in churches often broadly follows the prevailing artistic tastes in the surrounding area, and it is not surprising that a city such as New York boasts some of the more adventurous ecclesial art. Still, it is important not to make regional presumptions, and there is strong contemporary work being produced for institutions across the country. To note but one example, the Catholic painter Alfonse Borysewicz—who often takes inspiration from specific biblical passages and liturgical rites—has created an impressive body of work that hangs in churches, monasteries, and seminaries from Brooklyn to Grand Rapids.

Whether urban, suburban, or rural, congregations often struggle to find a balance between accessibility and innovation. This can be thrown into especially sharp relief when commissioning works on biblical subjects, which activate strong preconceptions. The process surrounding the construction and decoration of the Cathedral of Our Lady of the Angels (2002) in Los Angeles encapsulates this tension. After commissioning a daring architectural design from Rafael Moneo, the cathedral moved in a different direction for its interior, opting for explicit representations of holy personages, with clear references to the local community. From the architect's perspective, the cathedral's fear of art that might be labeled "in any way elitist" led to a missed spiritual and aesthetic opportunity.[20] For others, its conscious embrace of traditional Hispanic visual culture made the cathedral more, not less, modern. Ultimately, of course, each community must decide for itself how far to press its tastes, and where the greatest benefit lies.

---

20. Moneo, "Architecture as a Vehicle for Religious Experience," 168.

This tug-of-war between innovation and accessibility applies to syna-gogues as well, which must manage the same risk that art might be deemed elitist on the one hand, or banal on the other. But there are additional com-plications that Jews confront when creating works of art for sacred spaces. A key concern is how to interpret the Second Commandment, the so-called prohibition against "graven images" (Exod 20:4; Deut 5:8). While it is still a common misconception that the commandment prohibits visual art *in toto*, there is little basis for this in Jewish history or tradition, as scholars have demonstrated convincingly in recent years.[21] In practice, Jews have usually interpreted the Second Commandment permissively, and excava-tions of late antique synagogues at Beth Alpha and Sepphoris have even revealed lavish depictions of pagan gods. When it comes to synagogue art, one might even argue that modern designers have been more cautious than their ancient precursors!

While there are differences across denominations, contemporary Orthodox and Conservative congregations tend to shy away from human figures in synagogue art, and certainly anything that might risk anthropo-morphizing the Divine. Still, this reticence should not be confused with a lack of creativity. Indeed, such restrictions have at times yielded extraor-dinary results, such as Archie Rand's murals for the Orthodox B'nai Yosef Synagogue in Brooklyn and Adolph Gottlieb's stained glass windows for the Conservative Park Avenue Synagogue in Manhattan. Reform congrega-tions have taken the most widely varied approach to visual art among these denominations. In 2008, Tobi Kahn was commissioned to create eight wall-scale paintings and ritual objects, including the eternal light, mezuzah, and panels for the ark doors, for the sanctuary of Congregation Emanu-El B'ne Jeshurun, in Milwaukee, Wisconsin. To Dixon's question whether there ex-ists "a nonrepresentational art that is biblical,"[22] Kahn presents a compelling argument in the affirmative, conjuring mysterious forms—by turns cellular, geological, and cosmic—which channel the dynamic energy of Creation (Gen 1:1–3).

21. Bland, *Artless Jew*; Olin, *Nation without Art*.

22. Dixon Jr., "Bible in American Painting," 175.

FIGURE 1.3

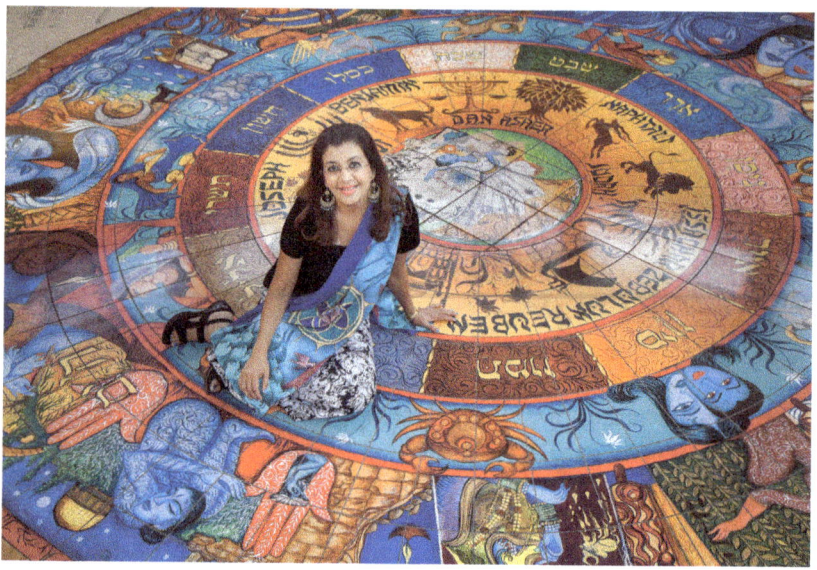

On the opposite end of the formal spectrum stands the tiled floor that Siona Benjamin designed for Central Reform Congregation in St. Louis, Missouri (2015) (Figure 1.3). Inspired by the zodiac mosaics of Beth Alpha and Sepphoris, the Indian-born artist created concentric blue circles which seem to oscillate like a whirlpool, swirling together biblical iconography with images from other faiths, including Hinduism and Islam. Rather than making the work less Jewish, this exuberant hybridity expresses a cultural openness that has become a defining emphasis of Reform Judaism in the United States.

After looking at the place of biblical motifs in religious institutions, it is time to turn now to a more ambivalent category: museums. The great museum collections of the United States, from the Metropolitan Museum in New York City to the National Gallery of Art in Washington, DC, are replete with works on biblical themes, mostly from pre-modern periods, when scriptural imagery was ubiquitous. While major national collections like the National Gallery do feature select modern works with biblical connections—such as Barnett Newman's magisterial *Stations of the Cross: Lema Sabachthani* (1958–1965)[23]—the Bible is rarely an emphasis in their modern holdings.

23. Dixon Jr., "Bible in American Painting," 178–79.

There are, however, a number of smaller museums that have sprung up in recent decades that have bridged this gap. On the campus of St. Louis University, for instance, Terrence Dempsey, SJ developed the Museum of Contemporary Religious Art in the 1990s by repurposing a Jesuit chapel. Meanwhile, on the West Coast, two seminal scholars of religion and visual art, Jane Dillenberger and Doug Adams, built up the Center for the Arts and Religion at Graduate Theological Union in Berkeley, which dedicated a gallery in Adams's memory in 2009.

Several museums specifically focus on the Bible and visual culture. The Museum of Biblical Art in Dallas was founded in 1966 but was recently reconstructed and expanded in 2010. On the one hand, the museum explicitly seeks to engage Christian visitors looking for a devotional experience, as in its Via Dolorosa Sculpture Garden. On the other hand, it endeavors to engage in interfaith dialogue through its National Center for Jewish Art, which collects works by contemporary Jewish artists including Tobi Kahn.

It is especially revealing to contrast the fates of two other biblical museums: the Museum of Biblical Art in New York City (MOBIA), which closed its doors in 2015, and the Museum of the Bible in Washington, DC, which opened in 2017. The curator Ena Heller opened a gallery space in the headquarters of the American Bible Society in 1997, which became MOBIA in 2005. As Heller explained in 2009, "To me the importance of the Bible is cultural and historic [and] the point that we're trying to make is that there's this one book that has influenced Western civilization more than any other book."[24] Despite this scholarly insistence on exploring the Bible's reception history, MOBIA still struggled—as Heller noted—under the assumption that it had "some sort of hidden agenda."[25]

If on the one hand MOBIA wanted to reassure secular audiences that it had no desire to proselytize, it also had to tread lightly concerning the missional work of its host organization, the American Bible Society, and also appeal to visitors and donors who wanted to see the museum embrace a more confessional approach to biblical subject matter. Treading this delicate line ultimately proved too difficult as the museum failed to establish secure financial footing to move into a new space.[26]

At the same time that MOBIA was struggling, the Museum of the Bible was consolidating its plans by actively embracing an evangelical agenda,

24. Rosen, "Unpacking the Bible."
25. Rosen, "Unpacking the Bible."
26. Kennedy, "Museum of Biblical Art."

spearheaded by its chairman and chief donor, Steve Green. Green is the founder of the Hobby Lobby supply chain, which in 2014 won the right to discriminate against female employees' healthcare based on the religious beliefs of the corporation's owners. Issues surrounding the Green family's religious and political agenda have been compounded recently by revelations about Hobby Lobby's illegal acquisition of artifacts from the Middle East.[27] Given this backdrop, it is an open question whether the Museum of the Bible can deliver on its stated educational and research aims in a way that is consistent with the standards of other museums in the capital.[28] It is also unclear to what extent the most adventurous contemporary artists, and those who own their work, will lend or sell to the museum; and if so whether the museum will have the stomach to display works which question the ideological commitments of the museum's leadership. While religious *criticism* has sometimes successfully threatened museums—as we observed in the first section of this chapter—it remains to be seen whether religious *support* is enough to overcome educational and curatorial concerns about a museum.

CONCLUSION

This chapter has surveyed some key ways in which the Bible appears in contemporary American art. While focusing on visual art has allowed us to contain an otherwise sprawling inquiry, it is important—in parting—that we do not ring-fence this category too closely. Visual art is but one dimension of the wider field of visual culture, and the Bible surfaces in every facet of this domain, from the content we browse on the internet to the television we binge watch to the leaflets we discover crammed into our mailboxes. Think, for instance, of the vast assortment of memes which have populated the internet in recent years, reimagining Donald Trump into biblical paintings (e.g., "Blessed are the poor . . . Wrong!"). Art does not exist in some sacrosanct realm, safe from the swells of everyday concerns. It bobs within the frothy, chaotic currents of visual culture. W. J. T. Mitchell asked in an important study of contemporary visual culture, *What Do Pictures Want?*[29]

The brilliantly simple question invites us to consider not only the complex demands we make of images, but the demands we allow them to

27. Zauzmer and Bailey, "Hobby Lobby's $3 Million Smuggling Case."

28. Museum of the Bible, "Research."

29. Mitchell, *What Do Pictures Want?*

make of us, through the culturally constructed act of seeing. In the context of the current inquiry, we might formulate a follow-up: What does the Bible want? Many Americans—too many, one might argue—think they know the answer to this question. Taken together, the first question helps destabilize the second. When the Bible becomes an image, it should give us pause. Even the most seemingly straightforward illustration makes additional demands of us. The best art today wants to interrogate our religious certainties, not confirm them.

2. Curating Interfaith Dialogue: An Exhibition as Pilgrimage

PILGRIMAGES ARE GOLD MINES for scholars of religious studies, replete with rich lodes of beliefs and practices.[1] When it comes to interreligious studies, however, the same sites are not so easy to quarry. The anthropologists Victor and Edith Turner got to the crux of the problem in their exploration of Christian pilgrimage in 1978, writing:

> With rare and interesting exceptions, the pilgrims of the different historical religions do not visit one another's shrines, and certainly do not find salvation *extra ecclesia* ... [Instead, pilgrimages] intensify the pilgrim's attachment to his own religion, often in fanatical opposition to other religions. That is why some pilgrimages have become crusades and jihads.[2]

The Turners' skepticism is warranted. In recent times alone, we might recite a tragic litany of pilgrimage sites that have been the subject of attack. The Harmandir Sahib, the Sikh Golden Temple in Amritsar, India has been attacked numerous times through its history, most infamously in 1984. The Cave of the Patriarchs in Hebron, Palestine—said to be the burial place of Abraham and Sarah and their descendants, and even Adam and Eve according to some traditions—has been a site of exclusion and violence over centuries, including a massacre of Muslim worshippers in 1994. In 2014, the tomb and mosque of the prophet Jonah in Nineveh, Iraq was blown up by militants of the so-called Islamic State as part of their devastating campaign against Muslim, Christian, and Yazidi holy sites in the region.

---

1. An earlier version of this essay appeared as "Exhibition as Pilgrimage: Visual Strategies for Interfaith Dialogue," in *Religion and Contemporary Art: A Curious Accord*, and I am grateful to the publisher for permission to reprint this adapted text.

2. Turner and Turner, *Image and Pilgrimage in Christian Culture*, 6.

Still, this lachrymose trail is not the only story one might tell. Indeed, the past decade has witnessed a flowering of pilgrimages devoted to interfaith worship, dialogue, and action. Some have taken the form of global summits, such as the pilgrimage convened by Pope Benedict XVI in Assisi in 2011, commemorating the twenty-fifth anniversary of the World Day of Prayer for Peace organized by his predecessor. Other pilgrimages have sought to shift popular perceptions about religion, especially in the wake of the "War on Terror," including a 2015 procession in London aimed at countering religious extremism and Islamophobia.[3]

In 2020, the murder of George Floyd, Breonna Taylor, and other African Americans by police unleashed a moral outcry for racial justice. Some pilgrimage sites formed spontaneously, sacralized almost overnight by the anguish and righteous indignation of protestors. The massive statue of Robert E. Lee in Richmond, Virginia—the former capital of the Confederacy—became a veritable shrine to Black Lives Matter, plastered with expressions of resistance and illuminated at night by a projection of Taylor, with candles and other objects arrayed at its base like *ex votos*. In Washington, DC, protestors for racial justice gathered at Lafayette Square near the White House—at least until they were forcibly cleared by order of Donald Trump—creating "a pilgrimage site of sorts," according to curator Aaron Bryant.[4] Formal pilgrimages took place that summer and autumn as well, including "Walk the Walk: A Faith Pilgrimage of Racial Reckoning, Resolve, and Love," from Charlottesville, Virginia to Washington, DC.[5]

Building upon long-standing efforts at the grassroots level, such endeavors signal a growing trend in which pilgrimages help symbolize, mobilize, and consolidate networks of religious activists working to effect social change.[6] Situated at the intersection of pilgrimage and protest, such

3. "Coexist Pilgrimage"; "Faith over Fear: Choosing Unity Over Extremism."

4. Bryant, "Curator's Corner."

5. "Walk the Walk."

6. Beyond self-defined pilgrimages, one might also expand this field of inquiry to include a range of mass political protests, stimulated in many cases by the election of President Donald Trump in 2016. To pick only examples from the left wing of the political spectrum—right wing protests have been larded with religious language and imagery, but very rarely with an eye toward productive interfaith engagement—one might include: the Poor People's Campaign, the Women's March, the March for Science, March for Our Lives against gun violence, and the Climate Strike, which have all had signature events in the US capital, as well as iterations across the country. While the formal agendas and demands of these protests have not usually been religious, they have—in different ways—constituted ritualized performances of identity, with significant implications for interreligious studies.

events provide ample avenues for interfaith dialogue. For my own part, as a scholar of religion and visual culture, I am particularly interested in the role that visual art might play in shaping participants' experiences of pilgrimage, especially in ways that motivate interfaith dialogue and action. In this essay, I want to focus on a single case study: *Stations of the Cross*,[7] an international, multi-site, public arts project I co-founded, whose mission is "to use the story of the Passion to prompt reflection and action in response to challenges of social justice."[8]

CONCEPT AND HISTORY

Stations of the Cross began as an exhibition in London in 2016. I then co-founded it as an annual project with the Anglican priest and theologian Catriona Laing, who became a key partner in developing the project, both practically and conceptually, in a way that made it adaptable across multiple countries and cultural contexts. While the project has evolved in scope and ambition, its guiding concept remains the same. The exhibition draws upon the devotional practice many Christians follow during Lent, in which they retrace the final fourteen episodes (stations) of Jesus' journey through Jerusalem, from condemnation to crucifixion and entombment.

In each city that hosts the project, curators design a bespoke, fourteen-stop route, marked by both existing and specially commissioned works of art. The journey—envisioned as a form of contemporary pilgrimage—weaves through both sacred and secular sites, and indeed often perforates the perceived boundaries between these categories. At every station, participants are invited to deepen their reflection by listening on their smartphones to specially recorded reflections by leading artists, thinkers, and activists. While rooted in Christian practice, *Stations* is designed to engage people of all faiths and none, with participating artists, podcasters, and institutions running the religious and cultural gamut.

One of the great learning experiences of this project has been the amount of negotiation it has required at every level, from the needs and concerns of artists to those of participating museums, churches, and other institutions, as well as religious, academic, and cultural funding organizations, each with their own remit. I have engaged in this delicate planning process—sometimes itself a form of interfaith dialogue—firsthand as a

7. *Stations of the Cross.*
8. *Stations of the Cross.*

curator for the project in London in 2016, Washington, DC in 2017, New York City in 2018, and online in 2021 during the COVID-19 pandemic. I have also had the opportunity to witness these engagements in an advisory role, as curators around the world implemented their own iterations, including: Amsterdam, NL (2019) co-curated by Marleen Hengelaar-Rookmaaker and Anikó Ouweneel-Tóth; Deventer, NL (2020) by Ouweneel-Tóth and Arent Weevers; Toronto, Canada (2022) by John Franklin; and Hengelo, NL by Weevers (2024). While I will focus on my own experience as a curator, I am grateful to these colleagues, who have brought their own creative vision to the project along the way.

Since this project is inspired by the Stations of the Cross as a religious practice, it is worth taking a moment to survey how this tradition evolved. The Stations have their roots in the Middle Ages, when interest in embodied devotion and reenactment of Jesus' suffering blossomed. The Crusades nourished—and were themselves fed by—a fascination with the specific locations associated with the passion. Over the centuries, veneration crystallized around certain key locations and moments in Jesus' final steps, moored less in Scripture or history than evolving popular tradition.

Indeed, following the surrender of the kingdom of Jerusalem to Muslim rule in the late twelfth century, the geographic Jerusalem began to pale in significance to the imagined Holy City, as creatively reconstructed in pilgrimage sites across Europe, from Italy to Ireland.[9] Christian pilgrims who did travel to Jerusalem in the ensuing centuries went looking for a city that had, in a sense, been invented in their own backyard. In turn, they superimposed this vision of Jerusalem onto the actual stones beneath their feet. Depending on whom one asked during the early modern period, the true *Via Crucis* could crisscross the streets of the Old City in any number of directions. And not only did believers wildly disagree on the number of stops to commemorate, it was even common for a period to retrace Jesus' steps backwards, starting with Golgotha, the site of his crucifixion.

The convention of reciting prayers at fourteen specific stations along the Way of the Cross in Jerusalem itself, or virtually at plaques erected inside churches elsewhere, was only formally established by the Catholic Church in 1731 by Pope Clement XII, with Franciscans playing a leading role in devotions. Even after this imprimatur was granted, innovation continued. In 1991, Pope John Paul II began celebrating an alternative fourteen-station "Scriptural Way of the Cross," linked more closely to the Gospels, which for

---

9. Turner and Turner, *Image and Pilgrimage in Christian Culture*, 6.

years he celebrated by walking around the Colosseum in Rome on Good Friday. While the Stations are most visible within Catholic practice and spaces, Anglicans and members of other Protestant denominations often follow their own iterations of the Stations, sometimes reducing the number to eight, for example, or highlighting episodes which resonate strongly with aspects specific to their theology or liturgy. In addition to denominational differences, diverse cultural settings—from the Philippines to Latin America—have also contributed to the ongoing development of the Stations of the Cross, sometimes incorporating practices from indigenous traditions.

As a curator, these myriad ritual, historical, and symbolic dimensions make the Stations of the Cross a uniquely compelling—yet also profoundly daunting—source to tap for interreligious dialogue. In the ensuing sections, I will consider how an exhibition explicitly inspired by Christian history and practice can enrich Christian observance while simultaneously providing avenues for deep but non-confessional engagement by non-Christians. I will focus on two, deceptively simple modes of engagement in which I think *Stations* fosters interfaith encounters and opens areas of inquiry for interreligious studies: looking and walking.

LOOKING

At its most basic level, the practice of praying the stations involves devoting significant time and mental energy to engaging with specific, physical images. This is a far cry from how most people engage with works of art in museums. Indeed, studies routinely show that visitors tend to spend mere seconds in front of even the most celebrated masterpieces. Alain de Botton highlights the dilemma facing curators in order to keep museums relevant and responsive to the emotional life of contemporary society.

"[A]rt museums," he opines, "often abdicate much of their potential to function as new churches (places of consolation, meaning, sanctuary, redemption) through the way they handle the collections entrusted to them. While exposing us to objects of genuine importance, they nevertheless seem unable to frame them in a way that links them powerfully to our inner needs."[10] The solution to de Botton's dilemma seems to stare him in the face, in his own framing of the problem. Yet rather than looking afresh at the myriad modes of religious viewing shaped and contoured over centuries, like the stations, de Botton hopes to reconstitute such experiences

10. De Botton, "Should Art Really Be for Its Own Sake Alone?"

through popular psychology. In 2014, he and John Armstrong selected and captioned more than a hundred works on display throughout the Rijksmuseum in Amsterdam, a repository of some of the world's finest religious treasures, including several biblically themed masterpieces by Rembrandt. For the title of this exhibition, de Botton and Armstrong boiled their thinking down to a single aphorism: *Art is Therapy.* This anodyne formula seems intended to apply to everyone, regardless of viewers' religious or cultural identities. And yet for an actual multifaith, multicultural, multiracial society jostling its way through the chaos and conflict of contemporary life, "therapy" feels like weak medicine.

We are better served, I think, by studying the complex, textured practices of "visual piety," which David Morgan defines as "the visual formation and practice of religious belief."[11] While earlier generations of curators expressly sought to avoid invoking such modes of looking, in the twenty-first century curators have begun—albeit tentatively in most cases—to embrace such connections. In a few cases, often as part of a strategy to engage specific local communities, museums have actually welcomed religious ceremonies in their galleries. For more than a decade, the Birmingham Museum and Art Gallery has hosted *Wesak* (Buddha Day) in its galleries, with devotions performed by Buddhist monks before the great copper *Sultanganj Buddha* (500–700 CE).[12]

For its part, Brighton Museum and Art Gallery has invited members of the local Gujarati community to perform *puja* at its historic Hindu shrine.[13] Wary of being construed as evangelizing, museums have pushed the boat out more cautiously when it comes to engaging the Christian liturgical context of many Western masterpieces. Neil MacGregor has been a pioneer in this field, overseeing the blockbuster exhibition *Seeing Salvation* at the National Gallery in London, staged in 2000 to coincide with the second millennium since Jesus' birth.[14] The show's design conjured an ecclesial ambiance through dimmed lights, dark walls, and liturgical music playing in the background. Yet despite such purposeful, palpable nods to

---

11. Morgan, *Visual Piety*, 1.

12. Paine, *Religious Objects in Museums*, 38.

13. Paine, *Religious Objects in Museums*, 39. As Paine reminds us, in addition to such museums "encouraging people to do religious things in their galleries," possibly more common "must be instances of people who pray, leave offerings, kiss icons or the like," which are not sanctioned or even recorded (40).

14. Subsequent shows at the National Gallery have built on this legacy, including *The Sacred Made Real* (2009–10) and *Devotion by Design* (2011).

Christian history and practice, the gallery delicately danced around the words *religious* and *spiritual* when describing its aims. The catalogue tellingly "expresses the view that modern secular audiences can engage with the masterpieces of Christian art at an *emotional* as well as purely aesthetic or historical level."[15]

Roughly a decade later, the British Museum—notably with MacGregor at its helm—staged a series of exhibitions delving into ancient Egyptian, medieval Christian, and modern Islamic religious practices. Rather than sheltering under the shibboleth of the "emotional," these shows sought to tackle devotion more phenomenologically, as part of a richly textured, lived religious reality. *Hajj: Journey to the Heart of Islam* (2012), curated by Venetia Porter, marked the culmination of this exploration. Viewers examined precious objects—including one of the world's earliest Qur'ans—alongside contemporary videos, soundscapes, and art representing the experience of Hajj today.

The exhibition unfurled along a spiral path through the museum's iconic domed reading room, evoking the centripetal procession of Muslims around the *Ka'ba* in Mecca. The exhibition was immensely popular across an audience that was 47 percent Muslim, compared to only 3 percent in a survey of general visitors the previous year.[16] A study commissioned by the museum found that a significant number of both Muslims and non-Muslims who attended *Hajj* reported not only increased knowledge about Islamic history and culture but "high levels of emotional and spiritual outcomes," with many citing the diversity of the crowds themselves as contributing factors.[17]

Running against the grain of much received museological wisdom, these findings suggest that it is possible to deliver satisfying pedagogical and devotional experiences simultaneously; and, indeed, that a complex interplay between them might be mutually beneficial. For an outsider, observing someone else's devotional engagement might be both educational and spiritually moving, while for an insider, watching an outsider thoughtfully delve into one's own tradition might prove both educational and uplifting. Where de Botton might rhapsodize about the potential for museums to become cathedrals, MacGregor's exhibitions remind us that if we want to *find religion* in museums, the answer may be confoundingly

15. *Image of Christ*, back cover, emphasis added.

16. Parker, "Museum Space as a Mediator of Religious Experience," 266.

17. Parker, "Museum Space as a Mediator of Religious Experience," 265–66.

obvious: we must do religious things there. And—just as importantly—do them together.

These lessons lingered with me as I planned *Stations of the Cross*, especially in its first iteration in London. From its inception, *Stations* was conceived not only as an opportunity to commission new works of art, but to reframe creatively how we discuss, experience, and interact with existing works of art. When working with contemporary artists, I have found that interpretive frameworks often evolve organically, alongside the creation and installation of their works. The non-Christian artists I have collaborated with on *Stations*, for instance, have displayed a remarkable openness to grappling not only with Christian themes and iconography, but Christian reception, including prayer.

I think in particular about how the Muslim artist Dua Abbas, the Sufi and Allevi inspired artist Güler Ates, and Jewish artists Leni Dothan and Siona Benjamin[18] embraced the challenge of presenting their work within explicitly Christian contexts, from the medieval Temple Church in London to the Cathedral of St. John Divine in New York City. In contradistinction, constructing a discursive framework around existing works has proven much more challenging, both rhetorically and bureaucratically. While artists may thrive in the uncertain territory of interreligious encounter, museums can—with good reasons—be squeamish about acknowledging religious and cultural difference; even, sometimes especially, when the religious (usually Christian) content of their collections stares one right in the face.

In her pioneering work *Civilizing Rituals*, Carol Duncan makes the case that public art museums in Europe and North America are "environments structured around specific ritual scenarios," which serve to inculcate and naturalize the ideologies of bourgeois nation-states.[19] While these rituals have shifted over time across different regional and cultural contexts, there remains a remarkable consistency in the rhetoric mustered to support them. "Advocates of art museums," Duncan notes, "almost always argue one of two ideals: the educational museum or the aesthetic museum," the first stressing the formation of informed citizens, and the second emphasizing the uplifting value of contemplation.[20] Despite their apparent differences,

---

18. See interviews and essays about Ates, Benjamin, and Dothan in Rosen, *Brushes with Faith*.

19. Duncan, *Civilizing Rituals*, 2.

20. Duncan, *Civilizing Rituals*, 4.

the former owing more to Enlightenment models of detached examination, the latter to Romantic fantasies of sublime encounter, "[b]oth ideals are advanced as *socially* valuable."[21] One key function—though Duncan does not dwell on it—is to underscore the beneficent religious tolerance of the state. The educational model brackets religion as a matter of mere historical interest. The aesthetic model, meanwhile, marginalizes it as merely personal reverie, disassociated from any particular creed (save that of *l'art pour l'art*).

Ironically, the "ritual scenarios" of the art museum thus seek to secure it a place outside the province of any definable, observable religious praxis, in service of an enervated—and many would argue, outdated—model of religious pluralism. For public museums, dependent in large part on public funding, adherence to this model is of vital, even existential importance. And so it is that even a modest curatorial intervention like *Stations of the Cross*, can in fact be controversial, simply by seeking to open space for devotional responses to art made for explicitly devotional purposes! In practical terms, this has meant delicate negotiations with senior museum staff about even seemingly tiny matters. At the National Gallery in London, for example, the museum's senior staff eventually had to sign off on placing a *Stations* wall text (with accompanying QR code) next to Jacopo Bassano's *The Way to Calvary* (c. 1544–5), linking it to the *Stations* podcast by New Testament scholar Joan Taylor.

In the end, the National Gallery set aside its concerns that offering such a conceptual framework might compromise its duty as a national institution to speak to viewers of diverse religious backgrounds. My clinching argument, made with the help of some theologically savvy curators, came full circle. *Stations*, I suggested, was simply extrapolating upon the logic of the National Gallery's own groundbreaking exhibition, *Seeing Salvation*. As that exhibition suggested, opening the door to one faith is sometimes the best, and most honest, way to invite discussions with others.

WALKING

It is not easy, as we have seen, to create an atmosphere, conceptual framework, or even physical space conducive to religious looking in public institutions, especially museums. Even if this can be accomplished, however, much more is required to make a meaningful pilgrimage. After all, a

---

21. Duncan, *Civilizing Rituals*, 4; italics in original.

pilgrimage is defined as much by its route—the spaces in between and along the way—as its destination. We began this essay with an admonition from Victor and Edith Turner about the challenges that pilgrimages, invariably geared towards in-group objectives, pose to out-group relations. It is telling, then, that as they describe the "liminoid" experience of pilgrimage,[22] and the profound feelings of interrelatedness it can engender—what they term *communitas*—they wonder whether such feelings might swell beyond the boundaries of particular faiths.

> [A pilgrimage's] posing of unity and homogeneity (even among the most diverse cultural groups) against the disunity and heterogeneity of ethnicities, cultures, classes, and professions in the mundane sphere—serves not so much to maintain society's status quo as to recollect, and even to presage, an alternative mode of social being, a world where *communitas*, rather than a bureaucratic social structure, is preeminent. Thus, out of the mixing and mingling of ideas from many traditions, a respect may grow for the pilgrimages of others. These may be seen as providing live metaphors for human and transhuman truths and salvific ways which all men share and always have shared, had they but known it. Pilgrimages may become ecumenical.[23]

At the heart of this reflection lies a crucial insight, not only for the study of pilgrimage but interreligious studies more generally: dialogue and camaraderie thrive on shared experience as much or more than shared theology. "Those who journey to pray together," the Turners add, "also play together in the secular interludes between religious activities,"[24] including a whole host of excursions off the religiously beaten track. The bonds that develop between pilgrims may, on the surface at least, have little to do with religion—an insight that dates at least as far back as the travelers in Chaucer's *Canterbury Tales*, swapping bawdy stories on their way to the shrine of Thomas Becket.

So how exactly does one go about planning a pilgrimage that walks this fine line between structure and liminality, between sacred and profane? As our exhibition has taken shape in each host city, my collaborators and I have focused first and foremost on assembling a coherent and compelling series of stations. At the same time, though, we have learned—sometimes

22. Turner and Turner, *Image and Pilgrimage in Christian Culture*, 35.

23. Turner and Turner, *Image and Pilgrimage in Christian Culture*, 39.

24. Turner and Turner, *Image and Pilgrimage in Christian Culture*, 37.

FIGURE 2.1

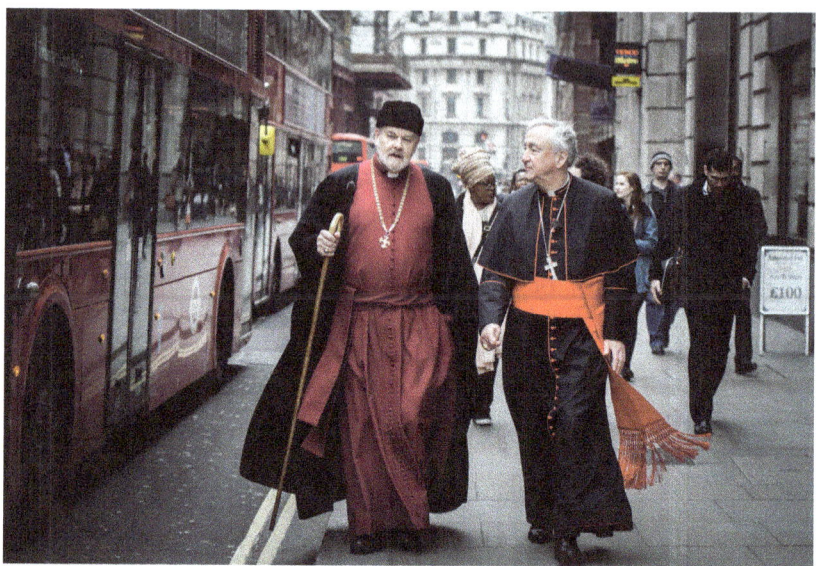

the hard way—that the project is most successful when it also values the interstices, drawing visitors along routes that are not only logical, feasible, and safe, but evocative in their own right.

We felt it was important from a practical perspective that stations connect in ways that would not require any particular navigational genius and could be visited in geographical clusters in case participants only had limited time or energy. Where possible, we considered areas congenial to multiple forms of transport, including bicycles, cars, and public transport.[25] But while our logo was inspired by the King's Cross train station, and participating artists have often explored the multiple meanings of "stations," walking has constituted an archetypal experience in the concept and design of the project. This is not without problems, and I am ashamed to admit that the ableism which this presumes entered my thinking later than it should have; not only because of the medical (and thus moral) importance of accessibility generally, but because the history of pilgrimage itself has so often been entwined with theologies of healing and wholeness.

25. There has been an interesting uptick in pilgrimages by bicycle, whether following traditional routes like El Camino in Spain, or developing new routes, such as Buddhist pilgrimages in California organized by DharmaWheels. There is also a growing literature about the psychological and phenomenological dimensions of cycling, e.g., Day, *Cyclogeography*.

FIGURE 2.2

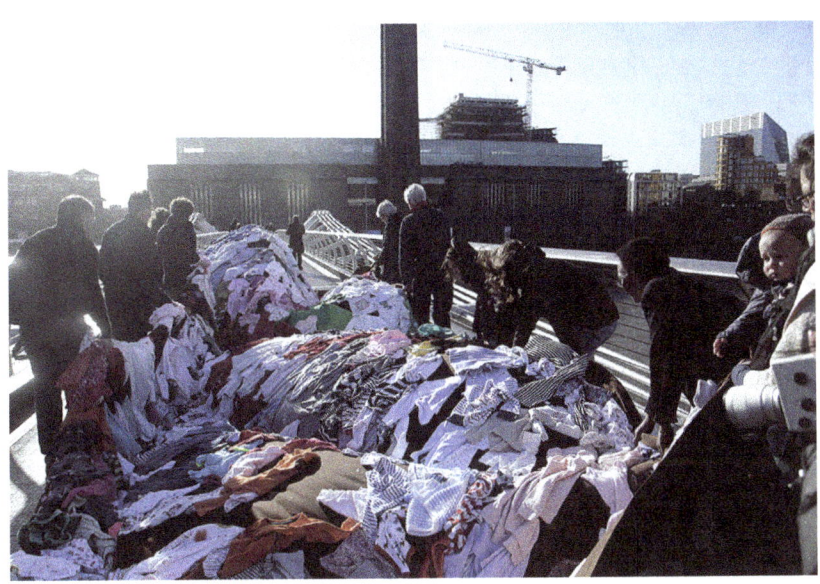

What has nonetheless kept walking, in one form or another, at the forefront of the project is a conviction that there is a powerful correlation between the pace of pilgrimage and its affectivity. At the most fundamental level, walking (or its aided equivalent) forces us to take things slow(er) and, in a deep sense, *to look where we are going*. In Turnerian terms, it promotes liminality, and the spiritual openness and attentiveness that comes with it.

As *Stations* has developed over the years, we have gotten better at conjuring the conditions for such experiences, whether by organizing walking tours or supporting partner organizations who do so. Sometimes these groups are specifically designed to promote interfaith engagement, like the walk I led with the Anglican Bishop of London Richard Chartres, and the Catholic Archbishop of Westminster, Cardinal Vincent Nichols, for *Stations of the Cross* in 2016 (Figure 2.1). At other times, ecumenical encounters spring up organically, when groups discover that they are traveling the same route, or pausing before the same work of art.

What is especially interesting, though, is the experience of solitary visitors who discover a sense of *communitas* along the way, with people they do not know, and may not even interact with directly. During *Stations'* first iteration in London, the religious studies scholar Brent Plate asked insightfully: "When people have to walk from one artwork to the next, how do you think their perceptions change? What's going on in that urban negotiation of crossing streets, and bumping against other people in between the more or less stationary contemplation of art?"[26] Still gathering data—and in fact still processing what the project was becoming—I responded rather speculatively:

> I like to imagine that at various points in the day, amidst otherwise indistinguishable crowds, there are people walking nearby—perhaps unaware of each other—taking this journey. And even if they aren't, I think it's a powerful idea to imagine that everyone we see walking anonymously alongside us might be a pilgrim, whether following these Stations of the Cross, or undertaking their own completely different journey.[27]

As it turned out, feedback via online surveys revealed that many visitors did feel an unexpected sense of togetherness during their experience. And this was especially noted by those who indicated that they had visited the *Stations* alone. "It felt like a pilgrimage and heightened my awareness to people around the walk, especially the homeless and disenfranchised in London and across the World," one respondent noted. "As a whole experience," wrote another visitor, "the walking through the city felt important; the seeking out being a necessary part of the task." One commented, "It was a remarkable experience . . . to reflect and to pray, all in the midst of the noise and frenzy of the city" before adding, "I wonder if worship spaces from other faith traditions might be incorporated as well?" Having self-conceived as pilgrims or seekers for the purpose of visiting *Stations*, it was clear that these participants began to see the city itself—and its extraordinarily diverse population—through the same lens. To them, it seemed, passersby were part of their pilgrimage, whether those individuals knew it or not.

My own moment of *communitas* came not while contemplating a piece of art, or walking between stations, but walking *with* a work of art. For the tenth station, in which Jesus is stripped of his garments, I commissioned the Turkish artist Güler Ates to create an installation for the Salvation Army International Headquarters' glazed lobby, visible from the street. Ates is best known for her photographs of mysterious figures in shimmering, diaphanous veils, drifting through opulent spaces. In *Sea of Colour* (2016) (Fig. 2.2), fabric took a different form, drawn from donated and discarded children's and baby clothes, too worn or damaged to be used

26. Plate and Rosen, "*Stations of the Cross* Exhibition in London," 255.
27. Plate and Rosen, "*Stations of the Cross* Exhibition in London," 256.

for charity. Working with a diverse assembly of volunteers including a local network of female refugees as well as members of the Salvation Army,
workers in the City of London financial district, and students of mine from
King's College London, Ates stitched the castoff clothes into a massive
tapestry dedicated to the millions dying and fleeing from the Syrian civil
war. Some items, emblazoned with animals, sports insignias, and holiday
designs, stood in mute testimony to stolen innocence, while others bore
messages of raw pain, inscribed by refugees. "Why did my son have to die?"
read a plain white onesie, scrawled with red pen.

Ates marked the completion of the piece with a choreographed procession, evoking Catholic and Orthodox rituals with icons and relics, including the Mandylion and the Veil of Veronica. The procession for *Sea of
Colour* began outside the Salvation Army, crossed the nearby Millennium
Bridge, turned around at the Tate Modern art museum, then retraced its
steps back to the Salvation Army, with the iconic dome of St. Paul's Cathedral rising behind. In effect, the route traversed the symbolic distance
between the realms of art and religion. The event began with a sinewy performance artist hoisting the massive tapestry over her head. As she trudged
forward, her shoulders hunched to bear its weight, the other volunteers and
I held the edges of the tapestry, like attendants lifting a bridal train.

As we marched, a few people in suits gruffly brushed past us. Some
tourists stopped and took photographs. But a surprising number of people
seemed to sense we were doing something important, however mysterious.
A few asked questions, then joined in as they grasped the concept, while
others helped silently for a bit without asking, then continued on their way.
It was a bright, chilly, cloudless day, but as we crossed the groaning suspen-
sion bridge the wind stiffened, catching the fabric. The tapestry began to
ripple, then violently crest and snap like ocean waves in a gale. The wind
effortlessly tore a half-dozen pieces of clothing from the surface, sending
them flying hundreds of feet downwind, into the river. It took the efforts of
everyone, including those recruited just moments before, to keep the entire
piece from taking flight.

As Ates later reflected, "The journey we took across the Millennium
Bridge was a very small reflection of the experience of modern-day refugees, who take extraordinary risks to reach a safer home."[28] In a poignant
episode of interreligious geometry, I found myself, a Jew, participating in a
performance led by an Alevi-Sufi inspired artist, commemorating both the

28. Rosen, *Brushes with Faith*, 129.

ancient suffering of Jesus and the present pain of Middle Eastern refugees. Rather than occupying the distanced position of a curator or scholar, in this liminal moment I had—almost without recognizing it—become a pilgrim.

CONCLUSION

"[F]undamental to every pilgrimage," writes David Freedberg, "is the element of hope."[29] Freedberg has in mind the soteriology of medieval Christians, seeking deliverance from misfortunes and maladies through the agency of icons and relics. Yet Freedberg's insight, I think, finds new relevance in the kinds of contemporary pilgrimages we have been discussing here, including *Stations of the Cross*. I imagine few if any visitors to *Stations* have gone looking to the art on display for palliative purposes, at least not physically. Nonetheless, visitor testimonials and survey responses from our host cities in the United Kingdom, United States, and the Netherlands have indeed registered an "element of hope" in other ways, most notably in their encounters with others.

Rather than preceding and animating pilgrimage, hope has itself become an outcome. This might not seem so miraculous—though I think we do well not to underestimate how remarkable it can be to find and sustain hope—but it has the advantage of being open and applicable to people across faith traditions, or even none. The acts of embodied looking and attentive walking that we have engaged with in this chapter are not the privileged holdings of particular faiths, however deeply individual traditions have explored their potential. For all their ostensible simplicity, such practices constitute a still under-utilized, under-studied resource for interreligious engagement as we march towards a more equitable future. Pilgrimages plotted and undertaken on these grounds may not save souls or heal bodies, but they may well repair communities.

---

29. Freedberg, *Power of Images*, 100.

3. Michael Petry's Old-New Paganism

WHAT HAPPENS TO OLD gods?[1]

As contemporary fantasy writers from Neil Gaiman to George R. R. Martin have surmised, they do not die easily, even when the cultures that invented them or the people that worshipped them pass away.

The mythologies of many ancient cultures bear witness to the messy process of discarding old divinities. The ancient Greeks, for example, inherited gods, stories, and symbols from Near Eastern cultures, which may explain their own obsession with myths of succession. According to Hesiod's *Theogony* (c. 700 BC), Zeus gained control of the heavens for the Olympians by overthrowing and imprisoning his father Cronus, leader of the Titans, who had himself deposed and castrated his father. Rebellion was in the immortal genes.

The Bible too retains traces of its convoluted heritage, strewn with references to divinities from other ancient cultures, from Babylonia to Egypt. Rather than presiding alone over the cosmos from time immemorial, the Psalms tell us that Yahweh "has taken his place in the divine council; in the midst of the gods" (Ps 82:1). For the ancient Israelites, whether their God was the only god was far less important than the fact that he was the greatest. Like any great characters—and the gods are some of humanity's very best characters—forgotten gods are ripe for resurrection.

Michael Petry is in the resurrection business. For the past decade, he has been busy fashioning ritual objects inspired by divinities from antiquity to the present. In his *Landscape of the Gods* paintings, Petry spells out the names of various heavenly realms, from Elysium for the Greeks to Vaikuntha in Hinduism and Jannah in Islam. The gestures and colors in these

---

1. A version of this essay first appeared in the volume *In League with Devils: Michael Petry*, and I gratefully acknowledge the artist's permission to reprint it here.

"landscape paintings" evoke the character of these empyrean destinations, sometimes with a cheeky edge. The famed fields of Elysium, for example, appear in radioactive green streaks, like a suburban lawn manicured to toxic perfection. In technique and ambition the works recall the mythic pursuits of the Abstract Expressionists, especially Barnett Newman. As Newman expressed in the Latin title of his monumental painting *Vir Heroicus Sublimis* (1950–51), "man heroic and sublime," he hoped to channel ancient virtues for a modern age. Long after this flush of postwar optimism has faded, Petry investigates for himself what we might salvage from long dead gods and ancient ideals.

How successful are such efforts? Petry gives us a clue in his installation *At the Foot of the Gods* (Figure 3.1), made from bronze casts of toes from contemporary sporting and cultural heroes. In a culture fixated on finding every icon's Achille's heel, there is a tenderness in Petry's works, lovingly

FIGURE 3.1

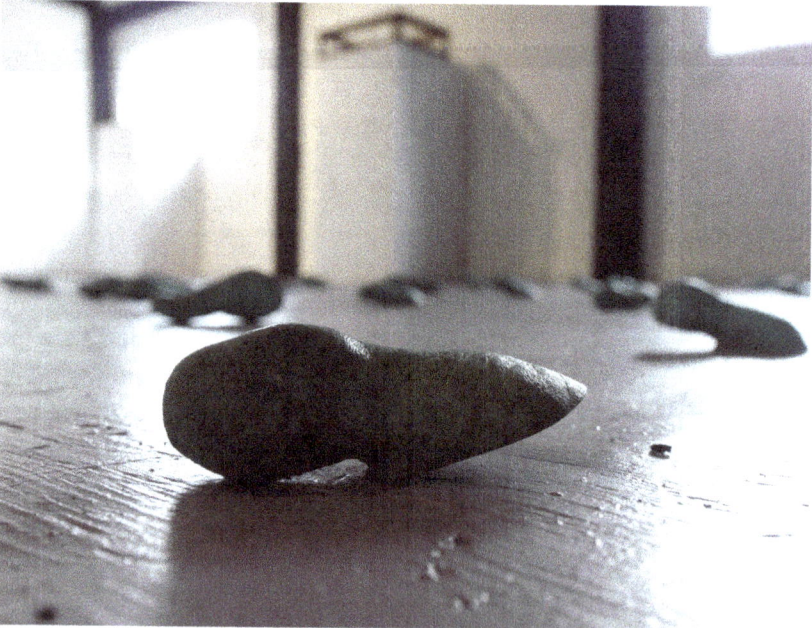

made by swaddling each subject's foot in silicone, a process Stephen Fry delightfully describes.[2] One imagines a ceremonial feel to such moments, akin to the ritual washing of feet on Maundy Thursday for Christians—in

2. Fry, "Foreword," 3.

memory of Jesus washing his disciples' feet (John 13:1–17)—or performing *wudu* (ritual ablution) before Islamic prayer. Casting these impressions in bronze might feel a touch idolatrous if these toes were to be enshrined on plinths, or the names of famous models proudly engraved beside them. But Petry wisely and poetically rests them upon the floor, like a pattern of precious pebbles found at the beach, or an array of offerings left in tribute to a god. The assembled digits manage to be at once precious and mundane, inviolable yet vulnerable, indicators of presence as well as absence. They do not allow us to see the gods in all their glory, but they do suggest we might touch their toes, or the hem of their garment, if we are lucky.

While we are reaching up to the gods, there is always a chance that they might be reaching down to us. To adapt a famous phrase from Rabbi Abraham Joshua Heschel, we might think we are the ones looking for God, but God is in search of *us*.[3] Petry is interested in gods of various types and traditions, but above all he is a devotee of Apollo, appropriately enough the Greek god of the arts. In *Gifts of Apollo*, Petry becomes a kind of servant of the god, crafting and delivering resplendent objects on his behalf (Figure 3.2). In doing so, Petry seems to provide the viewer with evidence of Apollo's presence, for only living gods bestow gifts. They become sacred objects

FIGURE 3.2

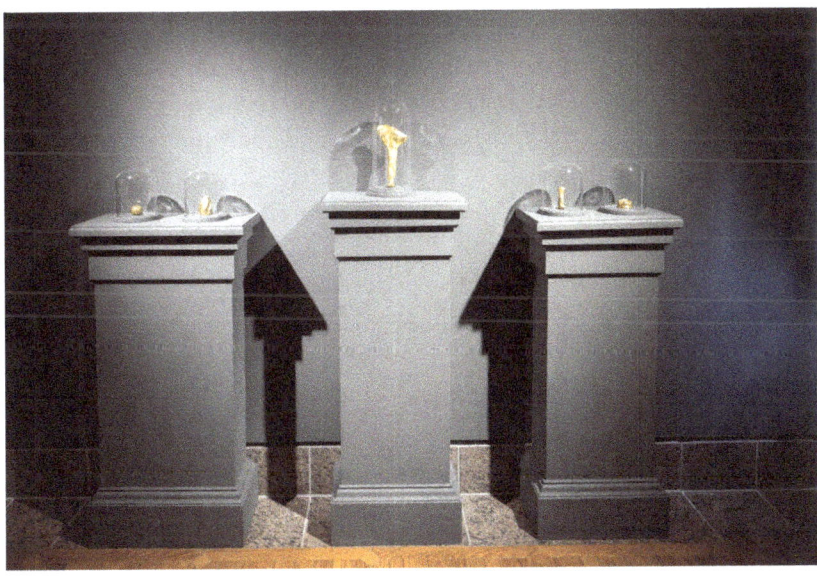

3. Heschel, *God in Search of Man*.

in the vein of *acheiropoieta* in Christian tradition: icons made without hands, pure impressions of divine presence. The indeterminate, allusive quality of these small sculptures underscores this otherworldly origin. Some suggest mysterious fruits, others the bones of uncertain beasts, even fragments of meteors from outer space. They sit naturally and proportionally in the palm of one's hand, as if made uniquely for us without our realizing it.

It is impossible for me to look at Petry's *Gifts*, or indeed this entire body of work, without being reminded of Rainer Maria Rilke's famous poem, "Archaic Torso of Apollo." Its opening stanzas read:

> We cannot know his legendary head
> with eyes like ripening fruit. And yet his torso
> is still suffused with brilliance from inside,
> like a lamp, in which his gaze, now turned to low,
>
> gleams in all its power. Otherwise
> the curved breast could not dazzle you so, nor could
> a smile run through the placid hips and thighs
> to that dark center where procreation flared.[4]

More than a century after its publication, we still do not know what precise sculpture Rilke was looking at when he composed these lines. But as a former secretary to the master sculptor Auguste Rodin, there has seldom been a viewer more attentive to the ekphrastic delights of describing sculpture. Rilke begins by asserting what "We cannot know," yet in the same breath provides us with the searing image of "eyes like ripening fruit." From a fragmentary torso, the poet-archaeologist confidently sketches every curve of Apollo's body, down to its "dark center." The sheer beauty of the sculpture does not merely entice or enrapture—though it certainly does both, as Rilke's erotic language makes clear—it issues a moral imperative. The last lines of the poem land like a lightning bolt: "for here there is no place / that does not see you. You must change your life."[5] As Rilke discovered through words, and Petry through images, Apollo does not have to be alive for his message to be immortal.

4. Rilke, "Archaic Torso of Apollo," 62.

5. Rilke, "Archaic Torso of Apollo," 62.

Making Memory

4. Contemporary Artists Confront Europe's Religious Heritage

"More great than human, now, and more August, / New deified she from her fires does rise." John Dryden wrote these optimistic words in 1666, in his poem "*Annus Mirabilis*: The Year of Wonders."[1] Only a poet of Dryden's immense imagination—not to mention a keen desire to please his monarch—could find signs of divine favor in that year, when London was struck by both the Great Fire and the Great Plague, all amidst a naval war. Writing under the long shadow of 2020—a year marked by its own pandemic, environmental catastrophes, and conflicts—it is hard to identify many blessings. Yet contemporary artists are already confronting the challenges rendered excruciatingly visible in this *annus horribilis*, and will continue to do so in the coming years. While few would opt for Dryden's theodicy, there remain good reasons to turn to the resources of religious heritage in order to formulate a vocabulary of lament, critique, and hope that befits the present. In turn, such efforts will reshape the contours of religious heritage for the future, in powerful but unpredictable ways. Without forecasting specific outcomes, in this essay I want to sketch out some key challenges I see at the intersection of contemporary art and religion, especially within a European context (although many of these challenges

1. Dryden, "*Annus Mirabilis*." This essay first appeared as "Art, Heritage, and Power" in *The Bloomsbury Handbook of Religion and Heritage in Contemporary Europe*, edited by Todd Weir and Lieke Wijnia. I am grateful to the editors for their input and Bloomsbury Academic for permission to reprint that essay here in edited form.

are global, and the implications will be as well). For heuristic purposes I will divide these challenges into subject, medium, and reception.

The great subject of art today, and certainly religious art, is power. If there was any doubt before, 2020 made this painfully clear, when the murders of George Floyd, Breonna Taylor, and other African Americans by police unleashed a moral outcry for racial justice. The raw anguish expressed in signs, graffiti, memorials, murals, and performances not only made powerful visual and ethical statements, but deeply religious ones, often channeling traditional iconography.

These interventions quickly spread beyond America. In Berlin, Jesus Cruz Artiles (a.k.a. Eme Freethinker) depicted Floyd on a section of the Berlin Wall in Mauerpark, in effect applying one critique of oppression to the embodiment of another. The art historian Nausikaä El-Mecky argues convincingly that the defacing and toppling of monuments also represent acts of profound moral and visual creativity, which should be seen in the context of events like the Iconoclastic Fury in sixteenth-century Europe.[2] In the United Kingdom, activists dragged the sculpture of slave trader and "benefactor" Edward Colston off his pedestal and (un)ceremoniously dumped him into Bristol Harbour. Not only was this act akin to performance art, it symbolically condemned Colston to the fate of the thousands of slaves who died aboard his ships.

Such public reckoning with the shameful, persistent legacy of European colonialism has injected fresh urgency into debates about objects of religious and artistic heritage stolen or otherwise dubiously acquired by European museums. French and German governments have made some strides towards repatriation of objects from former territories in Africa, but many activists remain dissatisfied with officially declared good intentions, and have taken matters into their own hands, such as the attempt to seize a Bari funerary pole from the Musée du Quai Branly-Jacques Chirac in Paris. Looking ahead, a central task will be not only how to recognize but sustain critiques of institutional racism. This will involve debates how best to preserve protest art (both *in situ* and in major collections), commission new public monuments, and incorporate critique into museums through revised pedagogies and interventions from contemporary artists.

While museums have a key role to play in such debates, so too do religious institutions, especially churches, which have often been willing collaborators in colonialism's mythmaking and exploitation. Contemporary

2. El-Mecky, "Spectacular Destruction."

FIGURE 4.1

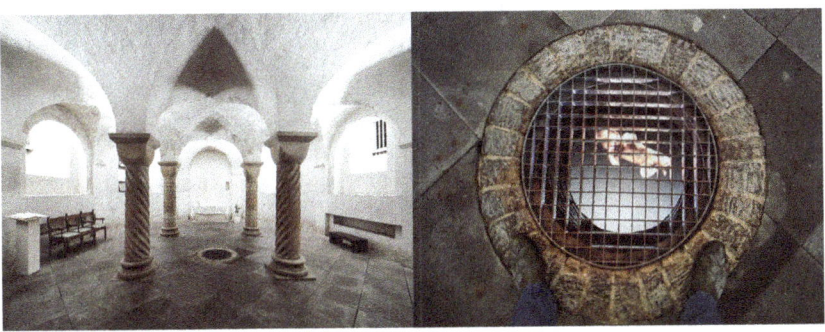

art, at its best, can help religious heritage sites morally disentangle themselves from the fabric of white supremacy, and build new forms of community in conjunction with activists and organizers. Theaster Gates's *Sanctum* (2015) provides a palpable example of what this might look like. Within the shell of Bristol's Temple Church—destroyed during the Blitz—Gates assembled a temporary chapel from discarded building materials around the city, which became a stage for twenty-four days of round-the-clock performances by local individuals and groups.

"In some ways this project was attempting to make space inside of a sacred space that people might connect with," commented Gates. "*Sanctum* is primarily a platform on which the people of Bristol have an opportunity to hear each other."[3] Projects like *Sanctum* offer a blueprint for how sustainable art and architecture can also foster more sustainable communities. As the twenty-first century progresses, environmental sustainability—including efforts to achieve environmental justice—will become even more crucial, and there is an opening for religious spaces to play a prominent role. Initiatives like Ocean Space, an "embassy for the oceans" supporting research and exhibitions, based in the Church of San Lorenzo in Venice, or the multi-cultural and multi-faith Gärten der Welt in Berlin, offer hopeful signals for the future.

As religious heritage sites hope to retain—or more optimistically increase—their relevance, many have turned to technology. Cathedrals and other large institutions, for instance, have increasingly employed smartphone apps for tourists to learn about their history, or splashed out for surround sound or high lumen projectors to embellish worship services. There has also been growing interest in site-specific works of art utilizing new

3. Klingelfuss, "Theaster Gates Hits All the High Notes in Bristol's Temple Church."

media. Bill Viola has been a pioneer in this field, creating a number of video installations for historic churches, as well as a permanent video altarpiece for St. Paul's Cathedral in London, entitled *Martyrs (Earth, Air, Fire, Water)* (2014). While the medium is bracingly contemporary, its polyptych format is centuries old, as is the artist's ambition for the piece, which he hopes inspires "traditional contemplation and devotion."[4]

Recently, another wave of new media artists has pushed the technological and conceptual horizons of ecclesial art even further. In the Netherlands, Arent Weevers has utilized virtual reality, holograms, and three-dimensional video, bringing cutting-edge digital capture and display to bear on abiding theological themes like vulnerability, grief, and responsibility. Drawing upon his expertise as a practicing pastor, Weevers has deployed a deep understanding of liturgical space to activate unusual features in heritage sites. In *Well* (2017; Figure 4.1), for instance, viewers peered through a grate on the floor of the crypt in St. Lebuïnus Church (Deventer, The Netherlands) in which a stereoscopic video played of an infant floating in a black void. While Weevers uses technology to bring singular, uncanny visions to life, Michael Takeo Magruder uses digital tools to analyze and visualize data in response to urgent social issues. For the historic St. Stephen Walbrook Church in London,

FIGURE 4.2

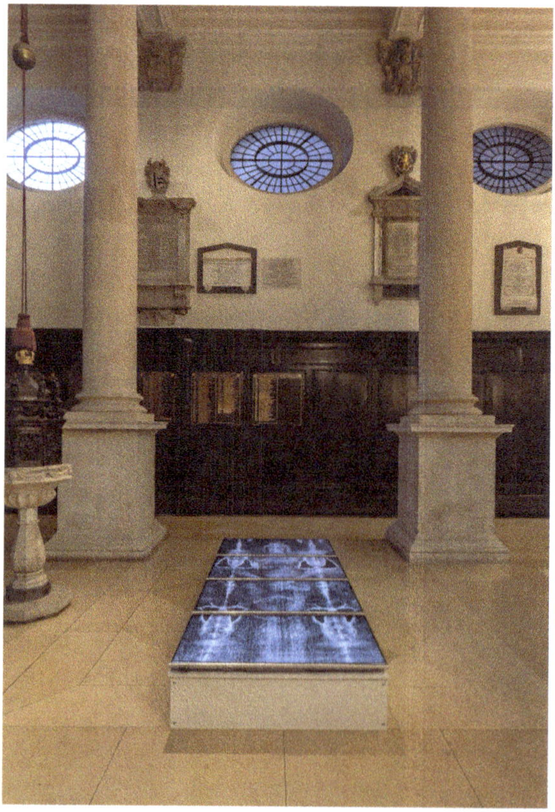

Takeo created *Lamentation for the Forsaken* (2016), a digital sculpture in which images of Syrian refugees gradually emerge and fade from the surface of a tomb-like structure, trading places, or indeed faces, with the visage from the Shroud of Turin (Fig. 4.2). The top, transparent layer of the piece is etched with names of some of the millions who have died in the Syrian civil war, in effect weaving together names and faces into a new shroud, a new icon. For all their formal differences, Weevers and Takeo each use the latest digital technologies in ways that spur deep reflection, especially about social responsibility. The challenge ahead, as digital technologies become increasingly affordable and accessible, will be for religious institutions to avoid using new media in merely opportunistic ways to refresh or update their offerings; or to put it biblically, pour new wine into old wineskins. Technology offers the most promise, aesthetically and theologically, when it is deployed by artists who appreciate the unique demands of religious spaces and respond to them—and the communities they serve—with sensitivity and imagination.

Museums, unlike most religious sites, have been displaying digital art and utilizing digital technologies for pedagogy for decades. Nonetheless, technology, art, and religious heritage can collide in fresh and challenging ways for museums, especially when it comes to reception. This was on full display in 2020 in a controversy surrounding mega-influencer Chiara Ferragni's photoshoot for *Vogue Hong Kong* at the Uffizi Gallery in Florence. When the Uffizi posted an image of her in front of Sandro Botticelli's *Birth of Venus* (c. 1485) on Instagram, its accompanying text suggested that Ferragni constituted "a sort of contemporary divinity in the era of social media." While the incident caused a *furore* among cultural commentators, for its part the gallery pointed to its spike in visitors soon after, many seeking selfies for their own Instagram feeds.[5] However unwelcome for the gatekeepers of religious heritage, the pursuit of the perfect selfie in front of a work of religious art might well constitute a form of pilgrimage; and in the hands of the right influencer might inspire untold numbers of "followers."

Rather than simply lamenting the fall of high culture and the depreciation of spiritual values, it is up to curators to generate additional modes of engaging religious and artistic heritage. One way to do so is by drawing inspiration from the tactile, embodied dimensions of looking that characterize the most enduring religious rituals. During the tenure of Neil MacGregor, the British Museum in London has offered compelling examples

---

5. For further discussion of this incident, see Rosen, *What Would Jesus See?*, 98–99.

of such an approach, with exhibitions that evoked experiences like praying before Christian relics in *Treasures of Heaven* (2011) or circling the Ka'ba in *Hajj: Journey to the Heart of Islam* (2012). It will be exciting to see how new generations of curators—including Lieke Wijnia at the Catharijneconvent Museum—build upon such trailblazing exhibitions. One challenge will be how to show contemporary works of art in ways that enable both piety and critique, or indeed one in service of the other. In an era in which artists are speaking publicly and persuasively about identities that have been historically suppressed or misrepresented in the art world, many changes may well be driven by artists themselves, who demand new forms of exhibitions. Recently, the Dutch artist Anjet van Linge has explored using medieval churches as spaces for open studios. She leaves me wondering whether one of the most important challenges ahead is not only how to get viewers to explore religious subjects or modes of viewing more deeply, but in fact experience religious making for themselves. As we move into an increasingly uncertain future, the historic rhythms and rituals of both art and religion can be precious sources of both stability and hope, especially when braided together.

5. Remembering the Witnesses: Jack Montgomery's *Soul Survivors*

THIS IS AN EERIE time to discuss Holocaust memory. Antisemitism is metastasizing in ways that many Jews, especially in America, hoped had long disappeared, or at least retreated into the margins. Instead, this ancient hatred seems to have a received a shot in the arm in the twenty-first century. In these conditions, the specter of the Holocaust feels more and more proximate, not just as a recent past but a possible future. As the organization JewBelong put it mordantly in a recent billboard campaign across America: "We're just 75 years since the gas chambers. So no, a billboard calling out Jew hate isn't an overreaction."

The resurgence of antisemitism comes at an especially precarious moment for Holocaust remembrance. The number of Holocaust survivors is dwindling rapidly with age, depriving us of firsthand witnesses just as their veracity and courage is needed most. What will the future of Holocaust memory be as we reluctantly envision a post-survivor era?

Some aspects are clearer than others. The personal burden of transmission will shift to second, third, and fourth generations who heard the experiences of survivors firsthand, or felt the weight of intergenerational trauma in their own lives, emotionally or even epigenetically. Official structures of memory have long been in place in institutions like the US Holocaust Memorial Museum in Washington, DC and Yad Vashem in Jerusalem, as well as numerous smaller institutions around the world, including the Holocaust and Human Rights Center of Maine. Yet they too will face new challenges as they seek to educate generations with vastly different habits and expectations for consuming information and building meaningful experiences. Creative responses to the Holocaust in art, film, music, and many other modes of expression will continue to germinate in the minds of those who did not experience the Shoah nor even know anyone who did, opening up fresh risks and possibilities along the way. The links in these chains of transmission will be tested in novel ways, especially in an online ecosystem of rampant disinformation, let alone deepfakes and other emergent dangers.

FIGURE 5.1

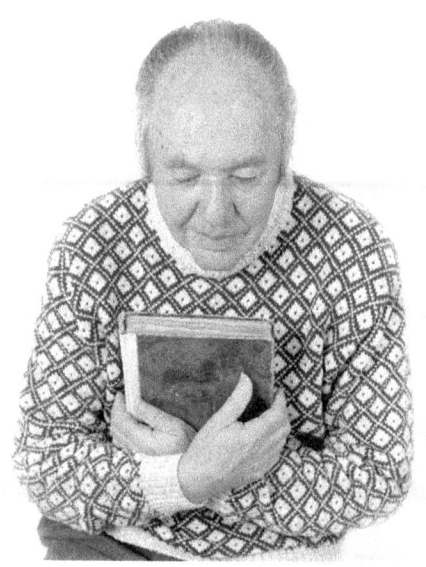

Looking at this uncertain terrain ahead, Jack Montgomery's *Soul Survivors* offers some important lessons. The project began with a series of tender black-and-white portraits of Holocaust survivors in Montgomery's home state of Maine (Figures 5.1 and 5.2), which have been exhibited around the state, including at the Maine Jewish Museum and the Holocaust and Human Rights Center of Maine (HHRC). *Soul Survivors* pairs these photographs with testimonies recounting survivors' lives before, during, and after the events of the Holocaust. They draw attention to the astonishing resilience with which survivors navigated the changed and decimated worlds into which they emerged. The relaxed yet unflinching gaze of the survivors—a testament to the close rapport Montgomery developed with his subjects—draws out this quality of quiet determination. While the focus of Montgomery's project remains squarely on preserving

FIGURE 5.2

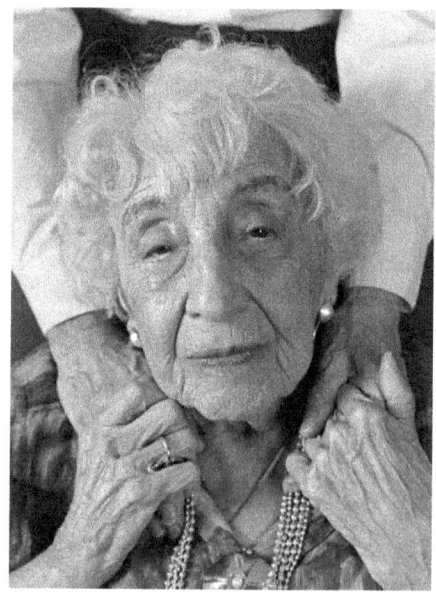

Holocaust memory, his eye for resilience has the potential to communicate across generations, speaking to multiple contexts. For young people, inundated with bleak projections for a climate-changed world, the defiant fortitude of survivors may sow seeds of resilience in their own lives, cultivating the kind of hope needed to create new worlds.

Refreshingly, Montgomery foregoes technical wizardry in his analog photographs. This is consistent with the ethos of the project, which emphasizes direct recollection, with little overt stylization. By working in black and white, Montgomery attunes viewers to a sense of historical context, inviting them to read the images reverently, with an attention to their artifactual quality. Of course, one must be on guard against simulating veracity, whereby devices like black-and-white photography or film merely serve to conjure the "feel" of truth. Montgomery navigates this dilemma by producing images which are deliberate, undisguised portraits. There is no pretense of happenstance. Individuals are aware not only that they are being photographed, but that their likenesses bear uncommon symbolic weight, inextricable from their identity as Holocaust survivors. If the unembellished character of the project feels somehow unfashionable, that may be just the antidote for media-saturated viewers. Rather than attempting to gamify the practice of memory, Montgomery takes both subjects and viewers with utmost seriousness.

The sincerity of Montgomery's project is not merely a formal attribute, it animates *Soul Survivors* as a whole. Throughout his career, Montgomery has turned his lens to those whom Jesus would call "the least of these" (Matt 25:45), people who have at one time or another occupied profoundly vulnerable positions, from young people undergoing transition in Maine to sex workers in the Dominican Republic. Montgomery's subjects are never simply passive; they cooperate in their own representation, revealing their intrinsic dignity in the process. Montgomery aims to commune with his subjects at an almost sacramental level. This means mustering the empathy and imagination to cross boundaries. He took on the project of *Soul Survivors*, for example, precisely because he was *not* Jewish—he was raised Episcopalian—and felt the imperative to bear witness to Jewish suffering.

Growing up in suburban New Jersey, Montgomery remembers one of the first times he heard about Jews. At a neighborhood gathering, someone told an antisemitic joke. Without hesitation, his mother turned and bluntly declared, "I'm Jewish," which she was not. In *Soul Survivors*, Montgomery channels that same reflexive impulse to identify with the Other, the person or group under attack.

This runs counter to so much progressive discourse around identity and discrimination today, which tends to emphasize the ineffable, incomparable nature of any community's experience to anyone outside that community. To do so, however, risks mystifying the suffering of the Other to the point that it becomes functionally impossible to bear witness to their suffering in tangible, meaningful, and enduring ways. Montgomery's project reminds us of the essential moral clarity which comes from deep, empathetic identification with others. Without practice, this skill atrophies, and antisemitism—like all other hatreds—thrives where moral imagination wanes.

6. The Kiln Decides: Trauma and Healing in Jesse Albrecht's Ceramics

POTTERS MAKE GOOD FATALISTS. In fact, the medium all but demands it. Even the expert ceramicist knows the most diligently crafted pot can still meet its demise in the kiln. An air bubble in the clay can burst like a bomb, taking its neighboring creations with it. A glaze can form an unsightly blister, or a sludgy glop on the shelf, requiring the potter to chisel it out. As a sign in a studio I frequented put it: "You make pots. The kiln decides."

Looking at Jesse Albrecht's pots, with harrowing images from his military service in Iraq, I couldn't help think of these words in conjunction with another, more mordant slogan: "Kill them all. Let God sort 'em out." The saying originated during the Crusades, when a Catholic general reputedly ordered the slaughter of an entire city in order to eliminate a group of heretics within. More recently, the motto has been appropriated by American troops. It captures the futility of discerning an un-uniformed enemy within a civilian population—from the Vietnam War to the "War on Terror" in Iraq and Afghanistan—and reaches a horrifying conclusion: it doesn't matter. The mention of God is hardly reassuring. He appears either as a cruel joke or an indifferent judge, bereft of mercy.

Albrecht is at home with these kinds of unsettling thoughts. Since completing his tour in Iraq, he has struggled with PTSD, which still leaves him prone to night terrors and startling at unexpected stimuli. In 2019, he spent seven weeks at an inpatient trauma recovery unit at a Veterans Affairs hospital in Montana. That space is depicted in the vase *Room 200, 2020* (Figures 6.1 and 6.2), produced the following year, which represents both a psychological and artistic breakthrough for the artist. At the base of the work, the artist's naked, tattooed body lies supine, in what yoga terms *savasana*, or corpse pose. From his mouth rises a giant crow, a key archetype for the peoples of the Northern Plains, especially the eponymous Crow Nation in Montana. Rather than a harbinger of death, as it is often read in Western culture, the giant bird seems to signal the potential for new life and wisdom, pulled from the jaws of trauma. It is fitting to learn that a sweat lodge ceremony, led by Native American veterans, constituted a turning point in the artist's recovery.

FIGURE 6.1

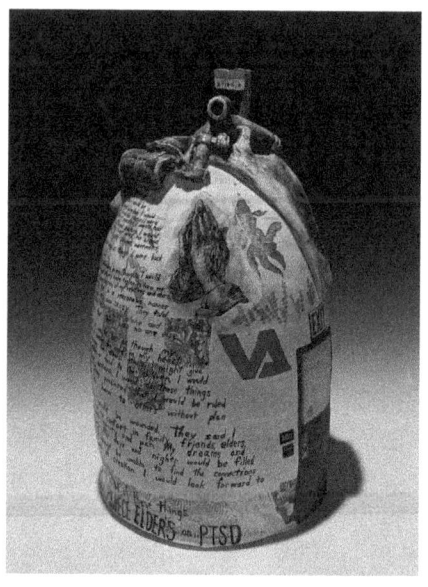

It would be reductive to label Albrecht's sophisticated ceramic practice—developed through years of training, including an MFA at the University of Iowa—as art therapy. Nonetheless, it has certainly provided an arena in which to excavate and process images and memories from combat. He writes:

> It can be very challenging revisiting the pictures from when I was there, reality and memory and dream gets all mixed up and it's like water and sun for the beast in me, he gets activated and I've used alcohol and drugs and adrenaline to sedate him. But I know forcing him to make art is the best.[1]

FIGURE 6.2

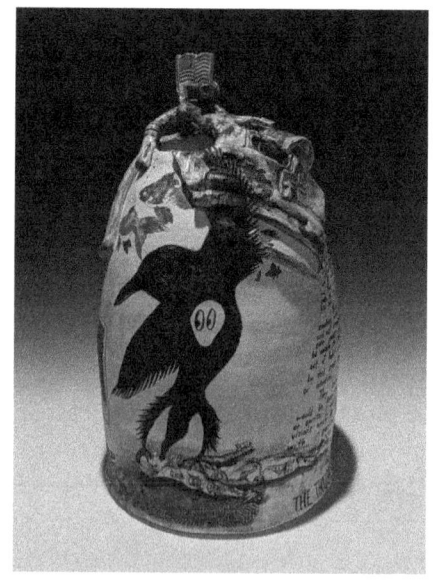

Religious imagery crops up frequently in this effort, drawn from a diverse array of traditions, from Shintoism to indigenous religions to Christianity. Within the latter, the eschatological conflict

1. Personal correspondence, February 2, 2022.

prophesied by the book of Revelation provides a recurring source. Albrecht intermixes references to the Beast, the Four Horsemen, and other iconic figures with reminders of more recent hellscapes, including the torture of Iraqi prisoners by US soldiers at Abu Ghraib Prison.

While these apocalyptic notes predominate, there are consoling images too, drawn from the mountains and rivers around his home in Bozeman as well as the history of art. In *Praying Hands* (c. 1508) by the artist's partial namesake, the German Renaissance master Albrecht Dürer, the ceramicist locates a sort of talismanic power. During his time "outside the wire," often positioned behind a light machine gun, he wore a necklace with these hands on it, engraved with the words "pray for peace." Later, Albrecht had the same hands by Dürer tattooed on his chest. Alternately traumatic and palliative, the images on Albrecht's pots jostle together like flotsam and jetsam, carried on the tides of the artist's unconscious. For his part, he seems to reserve judgment, as if to say: Let God (or the kiln) sort 'em out.

7. How to Curate a Dystopia: *Memory Palace* in London

THE TECHNOLOGICAL ACHIEVEMENTS OF the recent past have already become the stuff of hagiography.[1] After his death in 2011, Apple co-founder Steve Jobs reached a level of reverence usually reserved for the beatified. And like every saint, Jobs has his relics, including an Apple 1 assembled in his garage, which fetched nearly half a million pounds at auction. But what if all our computers—or indeed every digital device—suddenly shuddered to a stop, plunging the world into a dark age? What would we make of the carcasses of our precious iPhones, pads, and pods? Would they become sacred remnants or rubbish?

In the Victoria and Albert Museum's *Memory Palace* (June 18–October 20, 2013), the novelist Hari Kunzru and twenty collaborators from across the graphic arts conjure a dystopic future in which first the devices of memory, and eventually the act itself, are *verboten*. Less of an exhibition than an environment, *Memory Palace* envelops the audience, first and foremost, in a story. The opening wall text informs us that a magnetic storm has swept across the planet, leaving only the most rudimentary technology in its wake. Eventually, after several hundred years of enforced "Withering," all that remains of our era of "Booming" are half-remembered myths about the staggering, magical powers of "tricknology." Our protagonist belongs to a heretical sect of "Memorialists," who bravely transmit tales of the past under threat of death. After his arrest for belonging to an "internet," the Memorialist finds himself in a squalid, featureless cell. For his own survival, and that of the precious memories he has been charged with preserving, he

---

1. This essay originally appeared as "Remembering the Future in a Land of Forgotten Dreams," *Times Higher Education*, and I gratefully acknowledge the editor at that time, Matthew Reisz, and the publication.

imagines a "Memory Palace" crammed with holy fragments of history, science, philosophy, and art. Entering the show, we step inside the prisoner's head and into an uncanny "memory" of the present day.

The premise is original enough to be gripping, yet familiar enough to digest without too much exegesis. There are literary shades of Orwell, Kafka, and especially Borges, but there are also conscious nods to other media, including the graphic novel *V for Vendetta*, and Fritz Lang's visionary film *Metropolis*, from 1927. Rather than making *Memory Palace* derivative, these winks and nods cleverly mirror the plot itself, in effect recollecting and reassembling the genre of the post-apocalyptic itself. The structure of Kunzru's novella is likewise a pastiche of different styles, interspersing narrative sections with lists and other mnemonics, which often offer a dose of light relief. For example, we learn that "Old London" was comprised of a series of magnificent gates including Kings Curse, Use Town, Great Poor Land Street, The Edge Where, Notting Hell, and Waste Monster. With touching innocence, the Memorialist's dictionary tells us that "A bomb or boom was energy in a small space. In the beginning there was a seed or *paradigm*, which exploded, growing the towers and the hospitals and the bridges and pradas and ponzis."

Ultimately, the success of the exhibition hinges on Kunzru's ability to tread a middle ground between fragmentation and coherence. When co-curators Laurie Britton Newell and Ligaya Salazar first hatched the idea of the show, their guiding intuition was that they needed a writer willing to explore nonlinear forms of narration, which would nonetheless still revolve around a central theme. First and foremost, this bricolage allows readers the freedom to navigate their own route through the show, in essence assembling their own memory palace. Practically, Kunzru's bricolage naturally generated discrete, detachable segments, which the curators could snap apart and assign to individual artists or studios to re-present.

Crucially, this structure also allowed the curators to leave some passages out of the exhibition altogether. Newell and Salazar recognized the very real risk that the reader could be exhausted by the text, regardless of its quality. Rather than produce an awkward blend of book and exhibit, incapable of flourishing in either format, they opted to allow two projects to evolve out of the same genetic material. In its book format, Kunzru's complete text rightly takes precedent, interspersed with artists' working images. In the exhibition, the text is pruned down to its roots, allowing the images and objects to self-propagate. To borrow a phrase from Kunzru, a great interpretive "wilding" takes place.

To those acquainted with the terrain of contemporary graphic art, the list of artists involved in the project will read like an all-star cast of designers, illustrators, and graphic novelists. And while this certainly is not a survey show, one of the curators' aims was to draw from as wide a pool as possible, across multiple media and nationalities. Given this accumulation of talent, there is an extraordinary degree of humility that runs through the project. It begins with the curators' open brief to Kunzru, who in turn allows his text to be re-organized and re-interpreted by visual artists, who themselves manage to co-exist and cross-pollinate across creative boundaries. This ethos is reflected in the choice to avoid attributions within the exhibit, which—like most of the curatorial decisions in the show—emerges organically from the nature of the project. For some, this collaborative process already lies at the heart of their practice, especially the London-based artist collectives Åbäke and Le Gun. For others, the exhibition may very well be a breeding ground for future collaborations.

For sheer dynamism and delight, Le Gun takes the cake with an ambulance driven by a winged shaman and a pack of foxes, evoking everything from the sixties board game *Operation* to the prophetic visions of *The Seventh Seal*. The dizzying black-and-white detailing of Le Gun's fantastical chariot finds its counterpoint in Henning Wagenbreth's tower of brightly colored building blocks, playing on the prisoner's clunky definition of the museum as a place for musing and amusement. Each block has a different German or English word or phrase inscribed on every side, making the simple act of stacking bricks a complex exercise in language formation, as new shibboleths are coined and familiar expressions disrupted. The serious business of preservation and organization—the conceptual mortar of the museum—are but the flip side of creation and confusion. As Derrida would say, the Towers of Babel, *les Tours de Babel*, are also detours.

Sam Winston imagines a periodic table in which the elements have floated free from their boxes, swirling and recombining into mysterious new icons (Figures 7.1 and 7.2). Winston finds his inspiration in the Memorialist's statement that "In the ancient libraries and hospitals the alphabet marks were chanted as a prayer." Like all the prisoner's memories, there is a profundity in his error. Even as he distorts plain sense he transmits a deeper truth: in the words of Primo Levi, "formulas are as

FIGURE 7.1

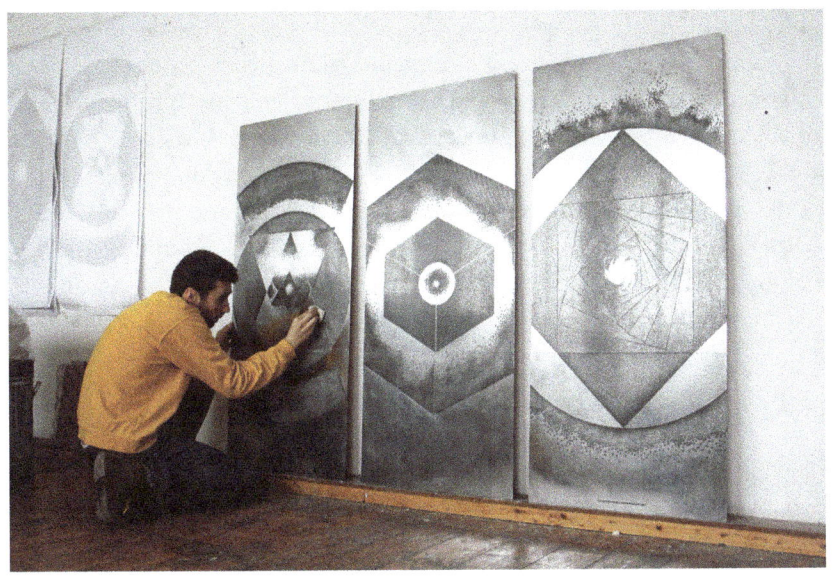

FIGURE 7.2

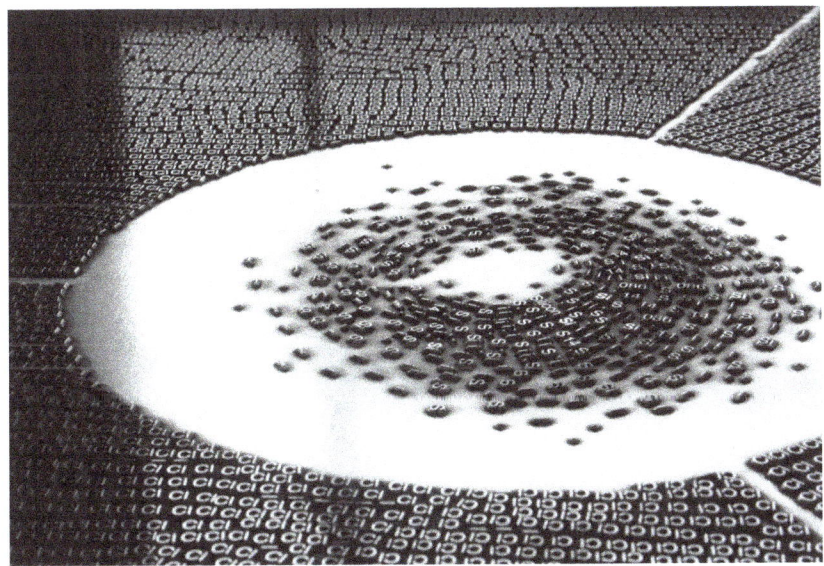

holy as prayers, decree-laws, and dead languages."[2] Winston's three metal plates—respectively embossed with the components of a SIM card, a watch, and a book—may no longer be legible as chemical formulae, but they evoke the yantra, tablet, and triptych of different faiths. Belief in one system has migrated to several others, leaving behind trace elements, or better yet, elements to trace. Seen through the eyes of artists, Kunzru's vision is perhaps not so cynical after all. "Despair is only possible when you have hope," he writes, but perhaps there is also hope in the charting and transmission of despair. Ultimately, *Memory Palace* is just as insightful about the future of culture as it is about the future of curation. To my mind, it is the most exciting curatorial experiment in recent memory.

2. Levi, *Periodic Table*, 203.

Navigating the Void

8. Picturing Nothing:
Finding Meaning in Monochrome

IS A PICTURE OF a boat religious? What if the boat in question is little more than a smudge? There are a number of works in *Icons: Worship and Adoration* that nearly all viewers will agree fit naturally in an exhibition about religion.[1] But Joseph Mallord Turner's *Sunrise, with a Boat Between Headlands* (1840–45) is a more curious case. Maybe it is the suggestion of first light that lends it a spiritual air. Or perhaps it is the intimation of a momentous journey just begun. Both may well be the case, but there is also another possibility. This work has been viewed as religious—and the same holds for many other canvases by Turner—not so much because of what *is* depicted but what is *not*. The gauzy, ethereal surface, especially when viewed from a distance, loses all distinction. More than it resembles a vessel leaving port, or indeed any other subject, one might make the case that Turner's painting is—to put it bluntly—a picture of nothing. And, paradoxically, this might be the most religious thing about it.

As the late curator Kirk Varnedoe reminds us in his insightful study of abstraction, what might appear to be "pictures of nothing"—the title of his book—may well be some of modern art's most profound offerings. In the history of art, he remarks, "we do not make things any simpler by making simpler things. Reduction does not yield certainty, but something like

1. The exhibition was held at Kunsthalle Bremen from October 19, 2019–March 1, 2020. This essay originally appeared in the exhibition catalogue, *Icons: Worship and Adoration*. I am grateful to the museum and publisher for permission to reprint it here.

its opposite, which is ambiguity and multivalence."[2] If this is true, there is potentially no more complex, no more meaningful, genre of modern art than the monochrome. For me, as a scholar of religion and visual culture, this ambiguity is precisely where things get interesting. On the one hand, the monochrome has been celebrated by some scholars and critics as a lofty pursuit of the sublime, the *ganz Andere* at its most beguiling. On the other hand, the monochrome has been interpreted as rigorously materialist, the purest possible investigation of the medium of painting itself. Depending on whom one listens to, the monochrome is thus either one of the most or the least religious motifs imaginable.

Let's begin with the latter. The formalist approach can be traced back to the great dogmatist of mid-century art criticism, Clement Greenberg. In 1955, in an essay on "American-Type Painting," he promulgated what he considered to be the defining features of modern painting. "It seems to be a law of modernism," he decreed, "that the conventions not essential to the viability of a medium be discarded as soon as they are recognized."[3] This "process of self-purification," as he imagined it, entailed paring away nearly every element of composition and technique, down to the medium's "viable essence" as a flat surface.[4]

Interestingly, Greenberg himself was hesitant to fully embrace monochromes—which flourished among American painters in the 1960s and seventies—as the natural culmination of his theories.[5] Other formalist critics, however, were more willing to celebrate the monochrome as the apotheosis of contemporary painting. Barbara Rose, a pioneering theorist of minimalism—married in the sixties to Frank Stella, who was painting flat gray works at the time—embraced the "unapologetic elitism" of single-colored canvases.[6] In her influential survey of the subject, which draws together insights from her earlier criticism, Rose presents the monochrome as a transcultural phenomenon. She argues: "The sex, nationality, race, and age of the monochrome artist are irrelevant and usually undiscernible."[7] Interestingly, religion does not even register in this litany of differences. The

---

2. Varnedoe, *Pictures of Nothing*, 56.

3. Greenberg, *Art and Culture*, 208.

4. Greenberg, *Art and Culture*, 208–9.

5. Staten, "Clement Greenberg, Radical Painting, and the Logic of Modernism," 75. Cf. De Duve, *Kant after Duchamp*, 251.

6. Rose, *Monochromes*, 82.

7. Rose, *Monochromes*, 82.

monochrome, as Rose imagines it, is the archetypal example of modernism's self-referentiality, in which aesthetics always trumps identity.

I am inclined to take a different approach. The ostensible purity of the monochrome, I would argue, only *appears* to mask the kind of specificities listed by Rose. What makes the monochrome so intriguing, and so ripe for religious reflection, is that it invariably fails to paint over difference, whether intentionally or not. Rosalind Krauss's remarks about grid paintings—a genre often overlapping with monochromes—are apposite here. She argues that artists ranging from Kazimir Malevich and Piet Mondrian at the turn of the twentieth century to Agnes Martin and Ad Reinhardt at mid-century used the motif of the grid to smuggle spiritual contraband under the noses of secular critics and scholars.

"The grid's mythic power," Krauss writes, "is that it makes us able to think we are dealing with materialism . . . while at the same time it provides us with a release into belief."[8] Spirituality, by this account, is repressed by the prevailing discourse of materialism, which converts modern art into "a secular form of belief."[9] Writing in 1978, when it was widely believed that organized religion was steadily melting away in the West, Krauss had every reason to suspect this condition was permanent. In the ensuing decades, this metanarrative has been progressively besieged, to the extent that materialism is no longer the dominant—or at least unchallenged—framework by which modern art is received and interpreted. From this vantage point, it is possible to see the monochrome, both in its past incarnations and its current permutations, in a new light, rich with religious resonances and implications.

SEEKING VOIDS

I would like to suggest some ways in which we might identify spiritual dimensions of the monochrome, concluding with a proposal that I think bridges the ostensible opposition between purely aesthetic and theological readings. When religious questions have been broached in relation to monochromes, they have often circled around the notion of aniconism. As David Freedberg defines it, aniconism is the "historiographic myth that certain cultures, usually monotheistic or primitively pure cultures, have no

8. Krauss, *Originality of the Avant-Garde*, 12.
9. Krauss, *Originality of the Avant-Garde*, 12.

images at all, or no figurative imagery, or no images of the deity."[10] Even when intended positively—as in the common (mis)characterization of Jews, Muslims, and Christians as "people of the book"—it can be problematic. While it may encourage some confraternity between the Abrahamic faiths, it simultaneously downplays, if not outright denies, the variety and richness of their visual cultures.

When applied to modern artists, the trope of aniconism invariably turns them into pious iconoclasts, regardless of their actual convictions and motivations. A case in point is Robert Pincus-Witten's claim that Mark Rothko's classic works derive from a "primordial consciousness of abstraction" rooted in the Second Commandment, the so-called prohibition against graven images.[11] The quasi-genetic terms of this argument—foisted on numerous Jewish artists over the years—are worrying enough on their own. But in Rothko's case it is particularly misleading.

Rothko's private remarks reveal that he only accepted the commission for his Houston chapel paintings—vast crepuscular canvases that verge on monochrome—because they were for a Christian institution. Not only was he keen to avoid being typecast as a "Jewish artist," he chose to actively invoke traditional Christian modes of contemplation, going so far as to select fourteen canvases—echoing the stations of the cross—and hanging them in triptychs.[12] For Rothko, the power of radical abstraction lay not in the deletion or denial of particular subject matter, but rather in the potential, given the right conditions and associations, to spark significant spiritual encounters, in the manner of the great religious masterpieces of the past. Rather than defining the monochrome by what it seems to renounce, we need an account which takes seriously what it presents; or, put another way, what it presences.

EMULATING ICONS

When painters have attempted to articulate this presence, they have often drawn comparisons to icons, especially in the Eastern Orthodox tradition. The analogy might seem surprising at first given the importance of figures in this tradition, from the Mandylion to Madonna and Child. And yet the

10. Freedberg, *Power of Images*, 54. For further context, see Rosen and Tabbaa, "Jewish and Muslim Art and Aesthetics."

11. Pincus-Witten, "Six Propositions on Jewish Art," 68.

12. Rosen, "Jewish Artists in Christian Spaces," 144.

stringent requirements of icon-writing, and the value it places on repetition, are echoed in the self-imposed strictures of many abstractionists, from Piet Mondrian to Barnett Newman. Still, no modern artist attempted to channel the aura and function of the icon as deliberately and doggedly as Kazimir Malevich. The Russian avant-gardist painted his revolutionary *Black Square* in 1915, which he later recreated in multiple versions, much like traditional icons. When first exhibiting the work in *0,10: The Last Futurist Exhibition of Painting* in Petrograd (St. Petersburg), Malevich hung the painting diagonally across the top corner of the gallery, in the location traditionally reserved for icons of saints in Russian Orthodox homes (Figure 8.1). Malevich even went so far as to stipulate that his *Black Square* be

FIGURE 8.1

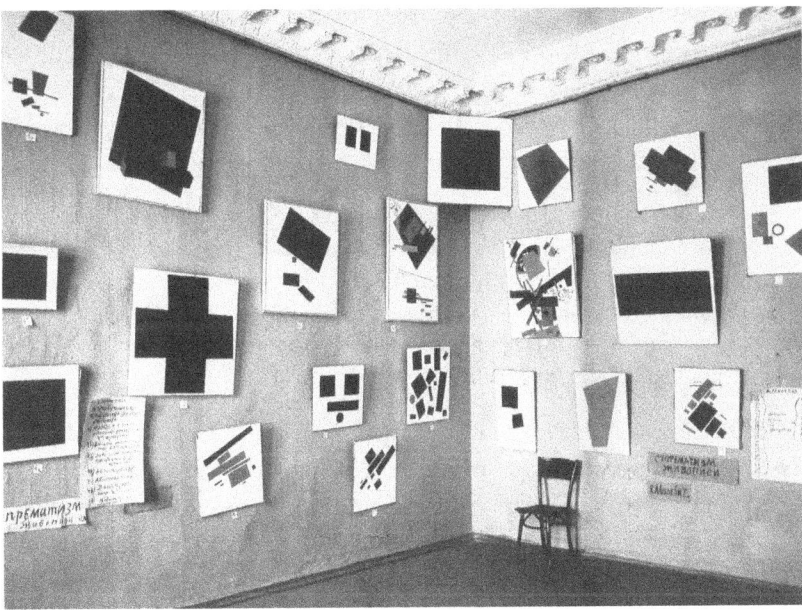

carried aloft at his funeral procession and placed above his self-designed casket in repose, further emphasizing its iconic function. With *Black Square*, and its austere companion, *Suprematist Composition: White on White* (1918), Malevich declared that he had reached the pinnacle of artistic creation, heralding the advent of a new spiritual age. Yet despite this pronouncement, Malevich eventually returned to making figurative paintings, furtively backdating them so as not to disturb his teleology. Here the problems with an iconic approach begin to surface.[13] If even Malevich, the great evangelist of the monochrome, felt such an unquenchable—even embarrassing—need to keep painting representational images, how can we expect viewers today to approach his black and white squares with the kind of uncompromising devotion he demands? The icons that weep, bleed, and heal the faithful have the advantage of belonging to a religious ecosystem, cultured over centuries. Without this religious context to stir spiritual expectations, even the boldest, most inspiring monochromes risk falling flat.

STAGING RITUALS

So how might monochromes, steeped in the culture of the avant-garde, stimulate such religious responses? One answer is for artists to generate this ritual significance themselves. For Yves Klein, the very matter of pigment itself constitutes a religious offering. In the winter of 1961, Klein quietly left a tripartite container of three pigments—pink, ultramarine, and gold—as an *ex-voto* at the shrine of Saint Rita of Cascia in Italy.[14] In the box, alongside several gold ingots, he placed a tiny handwritten note:

> . . . saint of impossible and desperate cases, thank you for all the powerful, decisive, marvelous aid that you have granted me up to now. Thank you infinitely. Even if I am personally unworthy of it, grant me your aid again and always in my art and always protect everything that I have created so that even in spite of myself it should always be of great beauty.

The phrase "in spite of myself" is not just a protestation of humility, it represents an ambition to create something beyond human capacity, something approaching the asymptote of the sacred. Klein's dedication evokes—consciously I suspect—the Christian tradition of *acheiropoieta*, icons believed by the faithful to be made without human hands. This desire to transcend artistry itself runs throughout Klein's works, especially the roughly 200 monochromes that he produced in his trademark International Klein Blue (IKB). Together, these works constitute what might be considered a single, sustained devotional practice.

A similar attempt to conjure the "*immatériel*," to use one of Klein's favorite words, animates the work of James Lee Byars, who often spoke

---

13. Pickstone, "Art's Last Icon," 109–18.

14. Restany, "Yves Klein e la mistica di Santa Rita da Cascia."

enigmatically of his pursuit of the "Perfect." Self-styled as a sort of *flâneur* cum mystic, Byars undertook performances that called attention to his eccentric persona—clad in gold lamé and top hat—while, paradoxically, attempting to diminish his very presence. In 1994, as his health began to fade from terminal cancer, he staged *The Death of James Lee Byars* in a Brussels gallery. If Klein sought to minimize the artist's gesture, Byars attempted to dematerialize the *body* of the artist. Lying motionless inside a giant gilded box, Byars seemed focused not only upon imitating but in fact becoming *acheiropoieton*.

Both Klein and Byars's monochromes seem to require an approach attuned to ritual action. They invite us to witness a discipline of disappearance. The question, ultimately, is whether these experiments encourage us to enter and participate in this ritual, or simply look on in wonder.

ENGAGING VIEWERS

Examining monochromes, and the discourses around them, has provided us with a spectrum of religious possibilities. When we turned our attention to the aniconic, we observed some of the dangers of applying a religious trope to artists simply by dint of their cultural heritage. Of all the reasons to paint a monochrome, it is revealing that critics frequently point to a strict adherence to Jewish, Islamic, or Protestant tradition, while artists themselves rarely do. Many more artists articulate a desire to create something iconic, not merely a monument to themselves but a work that emulates the affective power of a religious icon.

While an iconic approach allowed us to foreground the intention of the artist, however, it left unresolved whether such lofty spiritual aims could be fulfilled. Focusing on ritual allowed us to place the aims and experiences of the artist within a wider context, considering the monochrome not just as a singular phenomenon, but as part of an embodied practice, a religious as well as artistic discipline. The experience of the artist is, however, only half of the equation. It would be a mistake to assume that the viewer's experience simply mirrors that of the maker, with an artwork inducing the same ritual practice that engendered it. If the monochrome is meant to deliver a religious charge, the work must make a serious claim upon the viewer's attention and invite them into their own spiritual engagement.

What does this engagement look like for viewers? And, even more to the point, how does it take shape in a gallery, where one is most likely to find the kinds of audacious works we have been discussing? A traditional devotional experience is challenging, if not downright discouraged, by the conventions of museum viewing (touching the toe of St. Peter in his eponymous basilica is pious, rubbing the corner of a Malevich in MoMA is anathema!). This does not mean, of course, that an emotionally and spiritually affecting encounter is impossible in such spaces. James Elkins records a number of such occurrences, leading him to claim that "the majority of people who have wept over twentieth-century paintings have done so in front of Rothko's paintings."[15] More recently, Philip Francis undertook a sociological study of a surprising subset of individuals who have had religious experiences with works of modern art: evangelicals. Francis cites the case of Jakob Z., who had a rapturous encounter in front of Rothko's dusky Seagram mural paintings. Jakob recounts:

> There never would have been an undoing of my conservative Evangelical worldview without my encounter with the transcendent work of Mark Rothko on that rainy afternoon in London's Tate Modern. I sat there for five hours and everything came undone.[16]

Interestingly, Rothko's works opened a portal through which Francis's informant exited one form of religious identity into another; more uncertain for the subject, but ultimately more compelling. Such sublime encounters may well be possible in front of a range of monochromes, or similarly pared down compositions. But Tate Modern is not on the road to Damascus for most people, and it can be problematic to hold up limited experiences as a normative path for religiously engaged viewing.

A more accessible route towards religious experience may lie in the exertions—even the failures—of looking. The artist Ad Reinhardt seemed to sense as much. From 1960 until his death in 1967, Reinhardt fastidiously pursued infinitesimal variations on what he came to call his "Black Paintings." A gifted writer with a penchant for poetic manifestos—often brimming with paradoxes and neologisms—the artist outlined the concept and execution of these compositions as follows:

> A square (neutral, shapeless) canvas, five feet wide, five feet high, as high as a man, as wide as a man's outstretched arms (not large, not small, sizeless), trisected (no composition), one horizontal form negative one vertical form (formless, no top, no bottom, directionless), three (more or less) dark (lightless) non-contrasting

15. Elkins, *Pictures and Tears*, 4.

16. Francis, "Hand Outstretched in Darkness."

(colorless colors, brushwork brushed to remove brushwork, a matte, flat, free-hand painted surface (glossless, textureless, non-linear, no hard-edge, no soft edge) which does not reflect its surroundings—a pure, abstract, non-objective, timeless, spaceless, changeless, relationless, disinterested painting—an object that is self-conscious (no unconsciousness) ideal, transcendent, aware of nothing but Art (absolutely no anti-art).[17]

As Reinhardt's lectures and posthumously published notes reveal, he read widely in religious thought and philosophy from multiple traditions. He held a particular fascination for medieval and early modern Christian mystics such as Meister Eckhart, Nicholas of Cusa, and St. John of the Cross, who belong to the tradition of apophatic, or negative, theology. Rather than attempting to define what God is by affirming divine characteristics, apophatic theology seeks to establish what God is *not*. While Reinhardt would have chafed at being labeled a theologian, the language he used to describe Art—tellingly capitalized for him—was profoundly apophatic. Just as importantly, I would suggest, *the paintings themselves* speak apophatically.

Again and again in these works, Reinhardt carefully plots grids only to let them dissolve. He applies thin, almost transparent layers of paint all so that he might brush away his tracks. Every proposal in these paintings is erased, met by a counter-proposal. Stella, who owned one of these works, put it succinctly: "Those paintings are very hard to see."[18] The black paintings invite and require deep, sustained looking for the viewer to grasp anything. And yet they evaporate the moment one departs or loses focus, leaving behind no assurances, no certainties. Here, I think, material and religious accounts coalesce.

In the hands of a master like Reinhardt, the monochrome constitutes an extended experiment not only with the limitations and possibilities of painting, but with meaning itself. The viewer need not come looking for revelation—nor even find it—to participate in this spiritually significant act. The monk and theologian Thomas Merton, a lifelong friend of Reinhardt, had one of the artist's paintings in his hermitage. Perhaps he was looking at it when he wrote these words: "Do you think your mediation has failed? On the contrary: this bafflement, this darkness, this anguish of helpless desire is a fulfillment of meditation."[19]

17. Rowell, "Ad Reinhardt," 22.

18. Stella, "Black Painting."

19. Merton, *New Seeds of Contemplation*, 218.

9. The Face of the Deep:
Bosco Sodi Plumbs Creation

MORE THAN A PAINTER, it might be better to call Bosco Sodi a sculptor of paint.[1] He begins by stirring together a loamy mix of pigment, sawdust, glue, and water. Once the concoction acquires the desired consistency, he scoops it up by the handful and lobs it onto the canvas, creating strata upon strata of sediment. After hours of exertion, he steps back, leaving these creations to cure—sometimes for months on end—as their surfaces shift and settle along unpredictable fault lines.

Poring over the topography of such works, critics have unearthed a host of geographical and meteorological metaphors. To some, Sodi's surfaces suggest the parched beds of southwestern arroyos. To others, the fissures spidering across his canvases are evidence of seismic activity, whether tremors heralding "the big one" or craggy traces of some primitive eruption. When Sodi's palette shifts to blue, critics have spotted undercurrents, trenches, and floods, especially in the wake of Hurricane Sandy, when the artist's Brooklyn studio was inundated. In an era of exponential climate change, and disasters ranging from vanishing reefs to scorching wildfires and devastating hurricanes, Sodi's heaving color-fields feel equally ancient and contemporary.

While Sodi tends to leave his canvases untitled, when he has opted to christen them, he has favored words from the earth's primordial past, like *Pangea* (2010; Figure 9.1) and *Panthalassa*, named for the Paleozoic supercontinent and the ocean which surrounded it. The artist's evident passion for geology, biology, and chemistry is no doubt connected to experiments conducted growing up with his scientist father. And yet, Sodi's relentless

---

1. This essay originally appeared as "Monochromes and Monotheisms" in the catalogue *Bosco Sodi: Heavens and the Earth*. I am grateful to the artist for permission to reprint it here.

FIGURE 9.1

pursuit of origins and transformations—literal sea changes and tectonic shifts—strikes me, at its core, as profoundly theological. As much as he is fascinated by the factors that contribute to change, his deeper questions revolve around the very nature and necessity of creation. In the words of the medieval philosopher Thomas Aquinas, *creatio non est mutatio*, creation is not change, it is an act alone of its kind.[2] To apprehend the significance of this act, Sodi is no longer content to delve into the earth's prehistory. His most recent works seek to dig beneath time, to the moment of genesis itself.

How, one might ask, is it even possible to approach such a subject? Sodi does so by making decisions that are unprecedented in his oeuvre to date. While his paintings have, for many years, introduced variations in shades and hues—leading to soft striations and hazy plumes that subtly play across the canvas—Sodi has, for the most part, been a faithful monochromist. In this new series, he brings black and white together in the same composition, for the first time. Fields of ashen black and chalky white dramatically collide, generating some of the most defined forms the artist has yet created. Focusing upon this juxtaposition, probing the boundary between black and white—sometimes scumbled and permeable, sometimes strident and steadfast—allows Sodi to home in on the primary act of mark-making, with all the artistic and theological ramifications it entails.

In doing so, Sodi creatively looks back to his modernist precursors. We might think of Kazimir Malevich's *Black Square* (1915), which the Russian proudly considered a distillation of painting into its most essential, timeless form. Significantly, when first exhibiting the work in *0,10: The Last Futurist Exhibition of Painting* in Petrograd (St. Petersburg) in 1915, the artist hung

2. Thomas Aquinas, *Summa Theologiae* I, Question 45, Article 2, Reply to Objection 2.

the work diagonally across the top corner of the gallery (Figure 8.1). By positioning it in a location traditionally reserved for icons of saints in Orthodox homes, Malevich insisted—with all the zeal of a prophet—that he had fashioned not only an icon for the avant-garde, but the literal building block for a new age. Today, its eponymous square is covered with a delicate network of craquelure, lending the radical image the venerable texture of an Old Master. If one were to take a microscope to the surface, I suspect the result would be remarkably similar to one of Sodi's black-and-white paintings; the minute traceries of age turning to chasms upon close inspection. Like a pioneering atomic physicist or molecular biologist, Sodi reveals that even the most basic structure—a black square on a white canvas—contains still more fundamental units. There is a beginning to beginning.

If Malevich provides an entrée into structure, it is through the Abstract Expressionists that Sodi finds a lens to examine gesture in its most elemental form. Franz Kline used to say that he discovered his signature style of broad, sweeping black and white strokes by enlarging a section of one of his early paintings with a projector,[3] in essence launching his career through an act of self-exegesis, a search for the paintings within paintings. Just as Sodi could be considered an expositor of Malevich, one might also claim him as the rightful heir of Kline, seeking to isolate the primal energy that animates his predecessor's brushstrokes.

Alongside Kline, Sodi's images suggest a dialogue with several other painters of this generation, from the "firewritten" works of Morris Louis to the "white writings" of Mark Tobey. Or we might look to the surprisingly expressionistic brushwork in Mark Rothko's final acrylics, or the overtly calligraphic "burst" paintings of Adolph Gottlieb. Above all, though, Sodi's quest reminds me of what Philip Guston called his "pure drawings" from the late 1960s, as he transitioned from abstraction back to figuration. Consisting of a few deliberately crude brushstrokes of black ink on otherwise bare sheets of paper, these drawings "operate," as Michael Auping puts it, "at the very edge of description, a place where the abstract and the world meet, where the purity of the mark and the impure nature of recognition begin."[4]

As Guston was acutely aware, even a single, rudimentary stroke is an act of radical differentiation; the creation of *some-thing*, however humble, where before there was *no-thing*.[5] If this phrasing feels biblical, it is because

---

3. Perl, "Belated 'Breakthrough' to Abstraction."
4. Auping, "Impure Thoughts," 50.
5. Cf. Rosen, *Imagining Jewish Art*, 58–61.

the Bible itself describes Creation in terms that are irrepressibly artistic.[6] "In the beginning when God created the heavens and the earth, the earth was a formless void and darkness covered the face of the deep" (Gen 1:1–2).[7] With the instincts of a painter preparing a composition, "God separated the light from the darkness" (Gen 1:4); the first of many separations—heavens from waters, sea from dry land—by which God shapes the world.

Holiness, as Jewish tradition would later understand it, is inextricably linked to *havdalah* (separation), whether in terms of time, space, or community. By referring to "the heavens and the earth," Sodi not only invites viewers to see his paintings in light of Genesis, he beckons us to read between its lines, to explore the logic and implications of *havdalah*. Each canvas provides a new permutation on this principle, from passages of black that descend like dusk to ones which froth and swell like churning seas or lick the air like sacrificial flames (Figure 9.2). Sometimes light seems to divide the shadows, but often it is darkness that acts upon illumination.

FIGURE 9.2

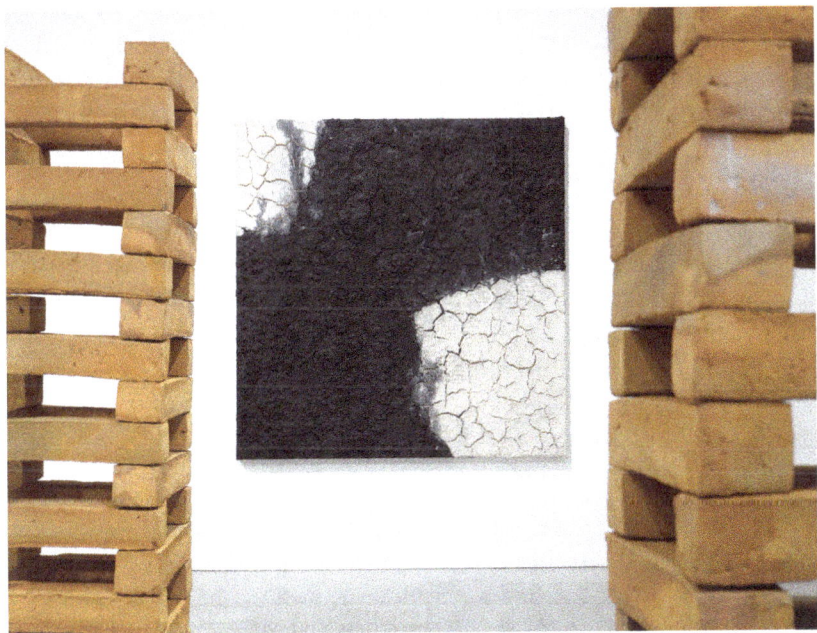

6. Raphael, *Judaism and the Visual Image*, 45. Cf. O'Kane, *Painting the Text*, 9–13.

7. All biblical quotations are from the New Revised Standard Version.

Sacred and profane engage in an unceasing dance, swapping values both chromatically and theologically. Holiness does not reside in one color or form over and against the other, but rather in distinction itself.

This oscillation between black and white, foreground and background, reminds me of a remarkable rabbinic tradition. According to the Jerusalem Talmud, the Torah—the Five Books of Moses—were "written with black fire on white fire"[8] before time began. The *text* of Creation, this mystical passage suggests, preexists even Creation itself. Scripture does not merely recount how light was divided from darkness, it *is* light and darkness. If we follow this paradox, divisions between text and image or scribe and artist collapse (to say nothing of time!). This tendency to hypostatize the text—to endow it with its own celestial presence—also surfaces in unique but related ways in Christianity and Islam.

The prologue to the Gospel of John famously asserts that "In the beginning was the Word [*Logos*], and the Word was with God, and the Word was God" (John 1:1). The Logos, which becomes incarnate in Jesus Christ, is a "light [that] shines in the darkness" (John 1:5). In Islam, meanwhile, there is a tradition that the pen (*Qalam*) was Allah's first creation, by which the world was written into existence. As Annemarie Schimmel explains: "Everything the Qur'an holds, has been written from all eternity on the *lauh al-mahfuz*, the Well-Preserved Tablet, by means of the preexistent Pen."[9] The world begins with inscription, in a sublime flourish of calligraphy.

I have suggested above that we might see Sodi's paintings as images that hover between the microscopic and macroscopic, enlarging the smallest brushstrokes in a Malevich or Kline into raw, crackling expanses of black and white. But perhaps Sodi's source material is something even deeper. If we look closely, maybe we might catch a glimpse—a single line of a single letter would suffice—of that fantastical *Urtext* blazing in the heavens. There is a Jewish legend that explains how even the miniscule embellishments atop a Hebrew letter in the Torah can carry extraordinary significance.

> When Moses ascended on high he found the Holy One, blessed be He, attaching crownlets [decorative squiggles] to the letters [of the Torah]. He said to Him, "Lord of the Universe, why should you bother with this!?" He answered, "There is a man who is destined to arise at the end of many generations named [Rabbi] Akiva b.

8. Ginzberg, *Legends of the Jews*, 1:1.
9. Schimmel, "Calligraphy and Islamic Culture," 107.

Joseph, [who will] expound upon each squiggle heaps and heaps of laws."[10]

Looking at Bosco Sodi's recent paintings, I like to imagine that I am seeing massive magnifications of just such embellishments, each inviting their own infinite interpretations. Perhaps, like the late, crepuscular canvases of Rothko, Sodi's works will eventually find their way to a chapel, where it is really possible to let these images work on the soul. For there is more than a touch of the sacred here. There are heavens made of earth.

10. Hayes, *Between the Babylonian and Palestinian Talmuds,* 18.

10. Mindful of the Gap:
Arent Weevers's Multimedia Installations

THEOLOGY AND ART ARE inseparable for Arent Weevers, like the braided wicks of a candle. His aesthetic and spiritual calling were kindled at the same time and grew from a shared dilemma. Near the turn of the millennium, Weevers began to feel frustrated with the limitations placed on him as a social worker, in which he could only work with the neediest cases for a handful of sessions. This anguish impelled him to seek other ways in which he might touch people's lives, beyond bureaucratic strictures. When he began theological training, he was—as he soon discovered—developing his artistic vocation as well. At their heart, both pursuits represented the search for a new language, capable of addressing people in pain in authentic, lasting ways.

Over time, Weevers began to develop a vocabulary centered on "vulnerability." He writes and speaks with unpretentious yet exquisite clarity about suffering, and the portal to understanding that it can provide, whether to oneself, the other, or indeed the divine. Stepping back to consider his life's work to date, Weevers reflects:

> The viewer often becomes aware of the irrevocable fragility of existence and of the unsolvability of your own suffering and that of the other. All in all, the viewer is asked to be daring and to contemplate it. You will be put on the track to God when you try to answer the call of the other.[1]

There is hard-won wisdom in these words, born of careful observation, listening, and service to others through many decades. Theologically, I hear echoes of some of the late twentieth- and twenty-first-century's most

---

1. Weevers, *Musings about Art,* 126.

sensitive thinkers on suffering, from the Jewish philosopher Emmanuel Levinas to the former Archbishop of Canterbury Rowan Williams. This diversity is not coincidental, for Weevers addresses pain in ways that do not depend on specific traditions—whether his own or his viewers'—instead plunging into the deep waters that run beneath and between traditions, common to people of all faiths and none.

Viewers will no doubt draw their own insights from this wellspring. For my own part, I am interested in the interpretive framework by which the artist is able to approach such daunting subject matter. It is telling, I think, that Weevers returns again and again to the word "vulnerability" when writing about his work. Rather than pain or suffering, which might be viewed from a more remote perspective, vulnerability—from the late Latin *vulnerabilis*, wounding—implicates us in a proximate, palpable, almost physical fashion. It speaks of pain that weeps like the stigmata, demanding that we minister to it (Figure 10.1).

FIGURE 10.1

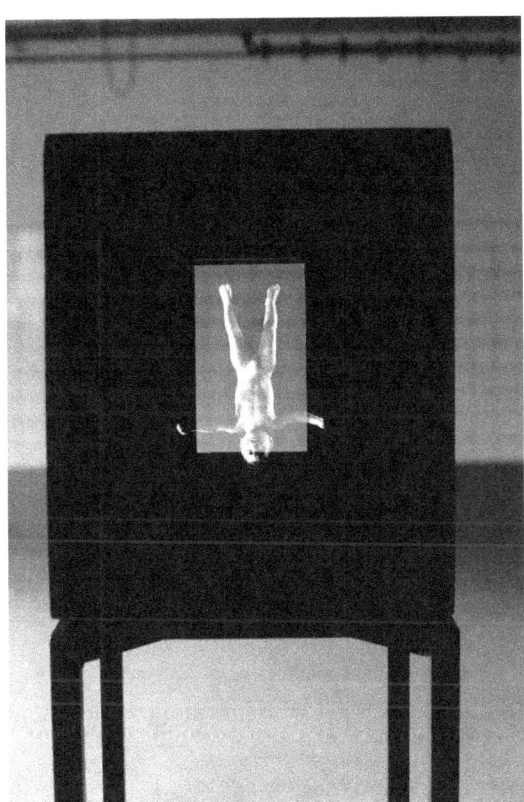

To see this raw vulnerability, beneath all the protections and artifices people construct to shield and obscure it, requires *attention*. Thinking about attention, I am reminded of the words of Weevers's countryman, the eminent if now rather neglected phenomenologist Gerardus van der Leeuw. Near the end of his magnum opus, *Religion in Essence and Manifestation*, van der Leeuw writes:

FIGURE 10.2

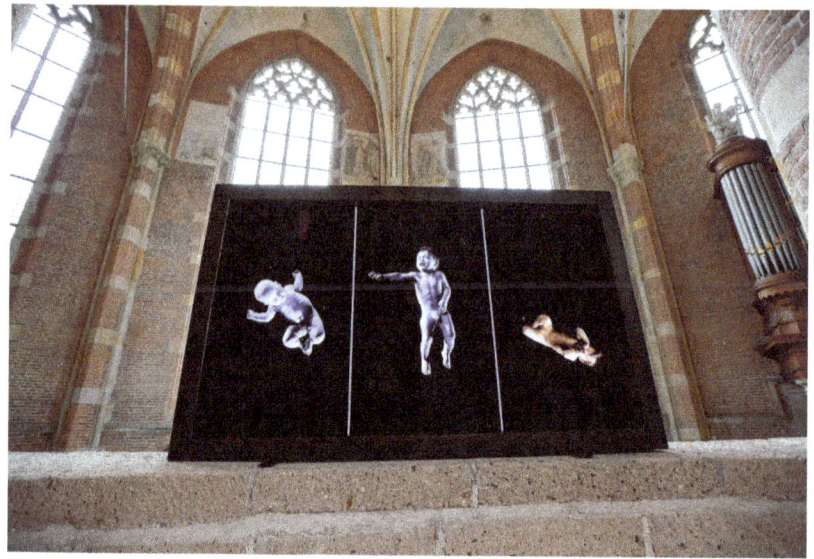

Understanding, in fact, itself presupposes intellectual restraint. But this is never the attitude of the cold-blooded spectator: it is, on the contrary, the loving gaze of the lover on the beloved object. For all understanding rests upon self-surrendering love . . . since to him who does not love, nothing whatever is manifested.[2]

Building on van der Leeuw's insight, I would argue that the kind of looking that Weevers's artworks encourage—and the kind he hopes viewers carry with them as they leave—is *loving attention*. He creates works that require this kind of consideration, schooling us in the art of compassion. After bearing witness to vulnerability through his crystalline visions, Weevers asks us to transfer this "loving gaze" to the messy world and people around us.

Weevers calibrates every aspect of his installations in order to sustain this mode of attention as long as possible. For all the variations in his compositions over the years, one recurring feature stands out, both aesthetically and conceptually. Weevers wants us to look long and deeply into the void. It is there in the cavernous interiors of the churches he prefers as venues; and sometimes even doubled, as in the black viewing cube constructed for *Josephine's Well*, or the grate that viewers peer down into in *Well*, located in the crypt of St. Lebuïnus Church in Deventer (Figure 4.1). Most of all, the

2. Van der Leeuw, *Religion in Essence and Manifestation*, 684.

void is present in the pervasive black expanse of so many of Weever's videos, in which his figures drift like astronauts untethered from their ships, or nocturnal swimmers in the inky deep.

This caliginous backdrop emphasizes the vulnerability of the figures, especially the infants who appear in several recent works, to the point that a number of visitors have expressed to the artist feelings of guilt or anxiety as they watch these children sink from view (Figure 10.2). But there is a further dimension to this void. Weevers muses:

> Vulnerability is about a 'gap' in concrete everyday life. 'Gap' because during this experience one realizes that man is not finished. It is an uneasy feeling. And we do all we can to prevent it. At the same time, precisely that is what connects people with each other: everyone is very deeply existentially vulnerable.[3]

The ubiquitous void, or gap, within Weevers' works turns out to be as much the subject of his work as the people suspended in its midst. Or, to put it another way, our loneliness—our desire for the Other—is made acutely manifest by absence. It would be easy to see this simply as a form of abandonment, both human and divine. And yet I think of the wisdom of Simone Weil, who had a preternatural grasp of the power and necessity of absence. "Grace fills empty spaces," she writes, "but it can only enter where there is a void to receive it, and it is grace itself which makes this void."[4] Perhaps the void is, in the end, a gift. If only we can muster the attention to recognize it.

3. Weevers, *Musings about Art, Body and Spirituality*, 90.
4. Weil, *Gravity and Grace*, 55.

PART II.
CONVERSATIONS

Sacred Geometries

11. Alyssa Sakina Mumtaz:
Stitching across Traditions

Alyssa Sakina Mumtaz is an interdisciplinary visual artist and educator working at the intersections of abstraction, sacred geometry, contemplative practice, and craft. Her work is exhibited and collected internationally and has been supported by grants and fellowships from the Pollock-Krasner Foundation, the Mass Cultural Council, and the New York Foundation for the Arts. She lives in Williamstown, Massachusetts, with her family.

Aaron: Your work weaves together references to both American and Islamic craft and visual art. Could you talk a bit about where you grew up and your religious and cultural landscape?

Alyssa: I grew up on a small farm in Maryland. I was raised outside of the framework of religion but absorbed my parents' nostalgia for rural American traditional culture. Being fascinated by early America and the idea of "living history," my mother taught herself to spin, knit, weave, and dye fibers. Throughout my early childhood she worked as a textile demonstrator at a local children's history museum, where I learned to weave on an enormous two-hundred-year-old floor loom. Looking back on these early experiences, I can clearly see the origins of my desire to jump over the generational ruptures that leave many of us feeling isolated from a deeper sense of tradition and identity.

Aaron: What were your first encounters with Islam like, and how did your decision to become a Muslim come about?

Alyssa: My first encounters with Islam unfolded through relationships— initially with my husband, a lifelong practicing Muslim born and raised in Pakistan, and later through a community of Muslim friends who guided and supported my transformation. On my first trip to Lahore in late 2009, I made the spontaneous decision to enter Islam while visiting the shrine of Miyan Mir, a seventeenth-century Sufi mystic. The *barakah* (blessing) of this early contact with the Sufi devotional ambiance has stayed with me over time.

Aaron: I'm interested in how that faith journey intersected or intertwined with your artistic path. When did you find yourself bringing motifs from Islamic sacred geometry into your work?

Alyssa: Sacred art offered me a profound early entry point into understanding spiritual practice. At the same time, engaging with its underlying philosophy precipitated a personal crisis. In the transitional period following my conversion, I kept my Islam mostly hidden, mainly because I wanted to shield it from misunderstandings that might throw me off course. Around 2013, I started to allow Muslim iconography to openly assert itself in my work. *Constellations* (Figure 11.1)—a series of intimate paintings on paper

FIGURE 11.1

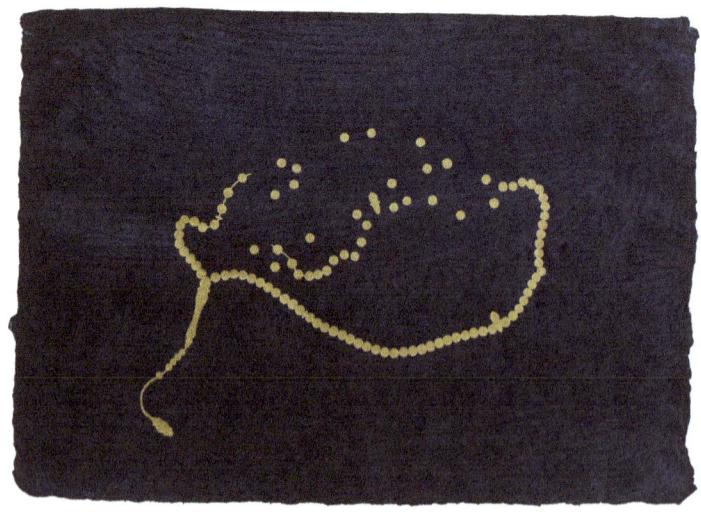

depicting the fluctuations of a single strand of Muslim prayer beads that I use daily—was the first project in which I attempted to represent the contemplative core of my spiritual practice. This body of work was also simultaneously a love letter to the many other religious traditions that utilize beads as a support for prayer. Engaging with the imagery of ritual paved the way for my embrace of sacred geometry, which became a more fully realized branch of my practice during the pandemic.

Aaron: How did you find viewers responded when these elements first started appearing in your work? Did you find you had to play the role of translator in some way?

Alyssa: Working through spiritual transformation in a semi-public way has been difficult at times, especially when playing the role of translator means defending the faith—or fending off the misguided idea that religious conversion is a form of cultural appropriation. In the secular social circles that I travel in here in the US—particularly the contemporary art world and academia—lived religious experience is a form of otherness that rarely gets the opportunity to speak for itself, unencumbered by politics. However, I have received a lot of support and encouragement when my work has circulated in Pakistan, India, and the UK—perhaps because religious expression is a less alien phenomenon there.

Aaron: We started by mentioning how you bring together traditional American and Islamic motifs. That comes out most in some of your textile pieces, which recall early American quilt designs and take the form of Islamic prayer mats. At a formal level, which motifs struck you as most adaptable and expressive across and between traditions? Were there specific regions or periods of American and Islamic design that particularly inspired you?

Alyssa: When people think of Islamic geometry, very often they envision complex, twelvefold star patterns intersecting with biomorphic arabesques and other mind-boggling feats of abstraction and resemblance. As much as I admire these possibilities within Islamic visual culture, my current practice draws from the multivalence of simple constructions (Figure 11.2)—namely, crosses and the eightfold stars that proceed from them. I love that these forms are transcultural (appearing independently in many contexts), richly associative, and open to metaphysical interpretation. When I look at

FIGURE 11.2

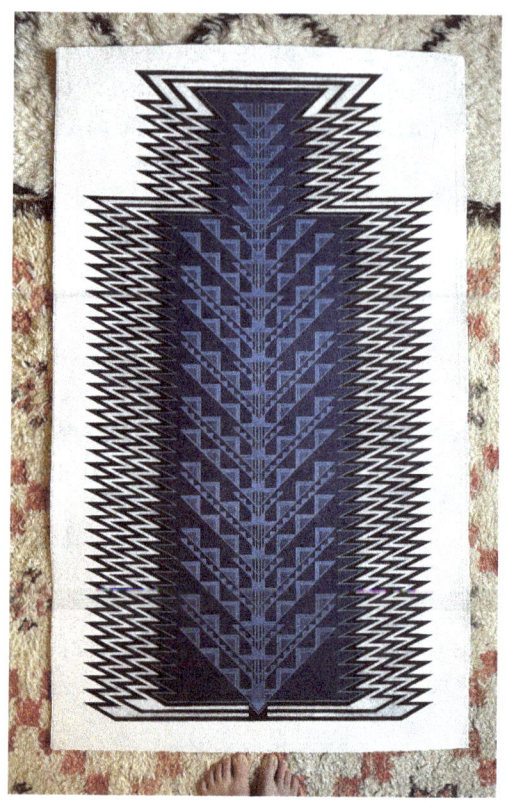

iconographic resonances between a traditional star quilt and a central Asian tribal prayer rug, I take it as one more proof that geometry, having no subjective, human author, is the underlying framework of divine manifestation. At some point, one must seriously ask, *why* do I see stars and crosses everywhere, across traditions? I would answer that these forms are anthropomorphic as well as cosmological, spatial as well as abstract. I look at so many things from various traditions, but recently I have been paying special attention to early American star quilts, the esoterically "revealed" gift drawings of Shaker women, and variations on the Indo-Persianate Hasht Behesht (Eight Heavens) architectural plan.

Aaron: Do you use any of the works you make in the home, or are they primarily destined for exhibition? How do you go about constructing sacred space in a domestic versus a gallery context, and what—if any—overlaps do you see?

Alyssa: After my children were born—and during the darkest days of the pandemic—I started thinking much more seriously about the boundaries of my life and what I hope to leave behind as a mother and artist. It occurred to me that the material archive generated by years of exhibition-making might become a burden for those who come after me. Bearing this in mind, I have consciously shifted much of my practice toward functional aims—namely, making art objects that serve a concrete purpose in the here and now of everyday life. The woven rugs and quilts that I make are meant to be prayed on and used in other practical ways. Anchored in geometry, my current drawing practice is alternately a form of study, a meditative exercise, or a design process.

I would never rule out the importance of exhibiting my work in public settings—bearing witness is an important dimension of how I see my vocation as an artist—but I do not prioritize public works over things that are more private, domestic, or ritual in character. Bringing these latter works into public space is a compelling but tricky endeavor. Recently, while exhibiting a quilted prayer mat at an art gallery in Karachi, I realized that it is almost impossible to hold space for the sacred unless a viewer is receptive to that dimension of the work—even in a place like Pakistan, where religion is such an assertive part of daily life. As much as one might try to include other people in one's worldview, they ultimately bring their own values and expectations to the experience.

Aaron: If you had to imagine the ideal setting for exhibiting your work, what would it be? And what kinds of spiritual responses might you hope to invoke in viewers?

Alyssa: Viewing art is the closest many people will come to having a contemplative experience. I am fascinated by the encounter between artists, artworks, and receivers, but I struggle with the conditions in which these encounters usually take place: emptied out, characterless gallery spaces; spectacle-like presentations that suggest entertainment rather than introspection; the cold, hard edge of capitalism. Instead of isolating my work from the various streams of spirituality, history, embodied knowledge, and lived experience that inform it, I want to be as generous as possible with viewers to ensure that they will truly receive something from me. I always welcome the idea of exhibiting my work in unconventional spaces that reflect the textures of my life—a barn, a decommissioned church, a historic rural home—as well as scenarios in which my practice might be understood alongside the frameworks and testimony of sacred art. If an encounter with my work helps a person's mind become quiet—even if just for a few moments—that is enough.

12. Askia Bilal: Patterns and Problems of Identity

Askia Bilal was born in New York City and is based in the Midwest. Working in acrylic, assorted dry media, and a method of collage that recycles his own paintings, he creates multilayered narratives that draw on a variety of artistic and intellectual traditions, with recurring themes of cycles, paradox, and layers.

Aaron: How has your religious and cultural background contributed to your work?

Askia: One of the primary forces that drives my creative practice comes from a belief that there is a deeper sense of purpose and meaning to life linked to a higher power. I use art as a tool to ask questions about that meaning, to make sense of the world and my place in it as a conscious being. Faith helps me grapple with the existential questions.

I experience Islam as a vast and rich tradition that flows from a Source from which other traditions have also emerged. Islam has encouraged me to reflect deeply, to ask questions, to gain appreciation for other cultures and traditions, to try to become more aware of myself, of others, of the Creator; all of these are essential to my work.

Aaron: Do you have any particular rituals when you're working in your studio, whether straightforwardly religious or not?

Askia: My routine in the studio varies. Sometimes when I get there I feel an urgency to work, and I can see clearly what I need to do and can even work on several pieces at the same time. Other times, I have to stare at a piece for a long time to determine how it needs to develop. The overall process of making art is ritualistic for me: I'm trying to access a greater rhythm, something larger than myself.

Aaron: How did the events of the past few years surface in your work, from the pandemic to the protests of police violence against people of color?

Askia: Both served as catalysts for my work. The pandemic disrupted all sense of normalcy and forced the world into isolation. At that time, I prioritized making art again, something that I had not done consistently for several years.

The murder of George Floyd and the subsequent protests prompted a new body of work called *Non-Portraits*, in which I began to address my experience of Blackness more directly (Figures 12.1 and 12.2). The *Non-Portraits* center Blackness in an effort to confront and deconstruct ingrained social conceptions of it. I'm negotiating a paradoxical space between invisibility and hypervisibility, the conscious and unconscious, portraiture and iconoclasm, figuration and abstraction. I've found this space where I weave together different strands of my identity and incorporate a range of references. Ultimately, I am trying to make archetypes that are windows to the mysteries of human existence.

FIGURE 12.1

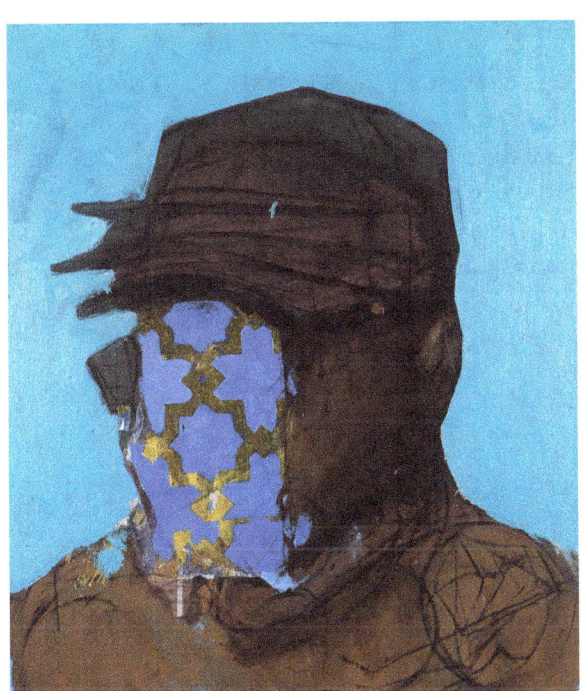

Aaron: In the *Non-Portraits* series, there are intricate geometric backgrounds that suggest motifs from Islamic art. Can you talk about the significance of those elements?

Askia: In general, the geometric patterns signify the infinite. They look as if they could repeat forever, which brings to mind all sorts of wonder—both within us and beyond us. They add a layer that enables me to dialogue with a tradition that I greatly revere.

Aaron: Who are some of the artists who influence you, past and present? I'm especially keen to hear more about the inspiration you find in Anselm Kiefer.

FIGURE 12.2

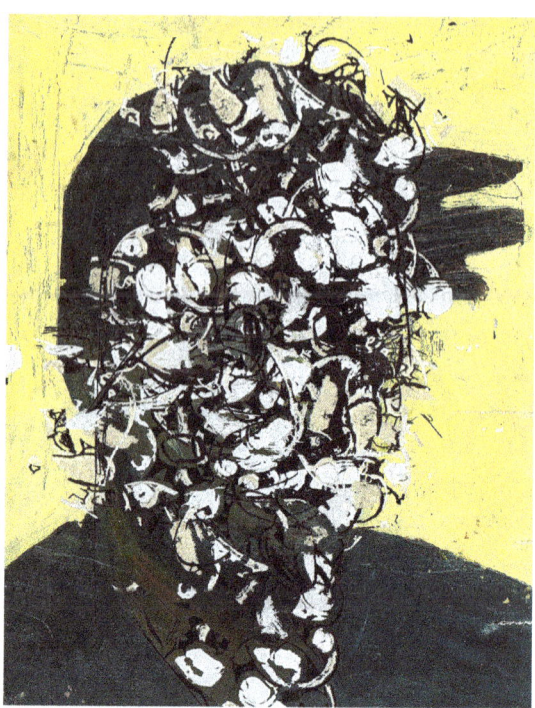

Askia: I am indebted to many artists; art does not happen in a vacuum. Some of my influences are Leonardo da Vinci, Willem de Kooning, Lee Bontecou, Jean-Michel Basquiat, Richard Serra, and Kerry James Marshall.

The first time I encountered Kiefer's work was as an undergraduate, when I saw *Breaking of the Vessels* (1990) at the Saint Louis Art Museum. I did not understand it and did not like it. When I saw it again years later as a more experienced artist, I felt the work immediately, and it had a profound impact on me. I recognize something in it that I have been attempting to communicate in my own work and voice. Kiefer's work evokes a sense of mystery, weight, and monumentality that resonates deeply.

Aaron: Thinking of *Breaking of the Vessels*, which is inspired by kabbalah, would you say there is a mystic element in how you create your work?

Askia: I'd like for my work to have a mystic quality. I think successful art draws you in and then holds you there, revealing itself over time in new ways. It can contain some transcendental truth. Successful art poses questions without providing clear answers; it makes people feel and contemplate, creating a space where they can be in wonder and become aware of something within and beyond the self. It awakens us to the world in a new way. I think mystery and awe are essential to the human experience, and art can continue to provide those things. If my work succeeds at any of the above for someone, I'd be content.

13. Armen Agop: Shaping Concentration

Armen Agop graduated from Helwan University in Cairo. In 2000, the Egyptian government awarded him the State Prize of Artistic Creativity, the Prix de Rome. After Rome, he moved to Pietrasanta, Italy where he now lives and works. He has won the Umberto Mastroianni Award and the Sulmona Prize, the Presidential Medal of the Italian Republic. Through his meditative practice in his work, Agop has developed a personal relation with matter and time, resulting in works that precisely describe ambiguous entities.

Aaron: How has your religious and cultural background contributed to your work?

Armen: Growing up in Cairo, Egypt (the land where monotheism was born and developed a unique heritage), in an Armenian family, I wondered from an early age about our beliefs, dreams, and how to perceive the universe. The cultural differences between my family's life and traditions and those of the culture outside led me to continually question values, and that led to a deeper search for the essential and the profound. It made me think about the fundamental needs of human beings.

Witnessing the monumental gods of ancient Egyptian art, which still hold a kind of sacredness even after their religious significance has faded, led me to research inner scale, to think about monumentality as something beyond merely size.

Aaron: Are there any questions you struggle with over and over?

Armen: I used to ask myself why humans go through sacrifices and insist on creating things that no one asked for or cares about. But not anymore. I realize that, in my case at least, it is simply an instinctive drive to *do*, and that's my way of being. When I am working, I am simply existing. By understanding that, I came to believe that art is beyond meaning. It transcends the individual and goes beyond you and me.

Aaron: How has your work changed in the past decade?

Armen: What has changed is the way I understand myself. I have more awareness of the simplicity of my instinctive drive. And then my way of working has become a more and more meditative process (Figure 13.1).

FIGURE 13.1

Aaron: What influenced you most in your formation as an artist?

Armen: Nature itself and the power of place. It was in the desert, where there appears to be nothing, that I learned to see. The dunes slowly transform in an endless communication between wind and sand (Figure 13.2). The lines on the crests of the dunes sharpen and mellow as the landscape continuously shifts. Rather than boredom, there is a sense of deep familiarity, of existing and preexisting through time. It is a familiarity not only with the landscape but with ourselves, with our capacity to unite with the changing universe inside and outside of us.

FIGURE 13.2

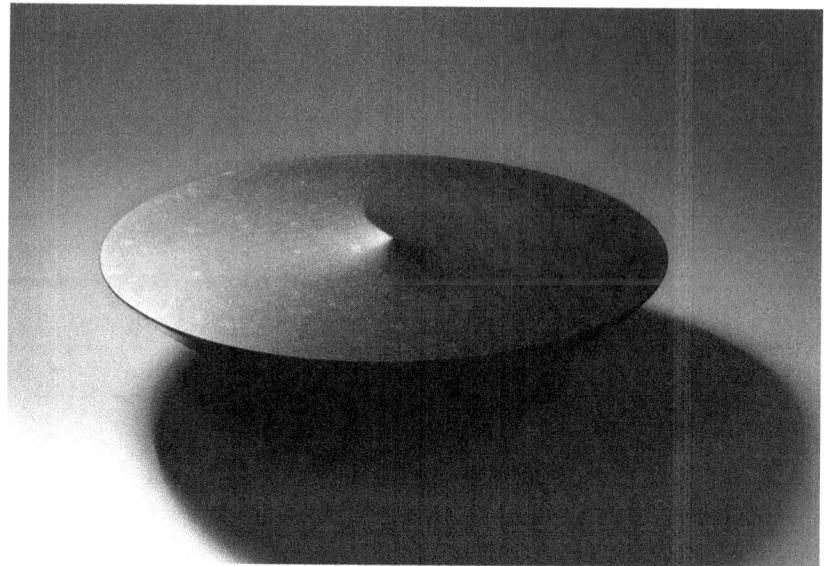

Aaron: Do you notice people respond differently to your work in different countries and settings?

Armen: Every culture reflects itself in what they do and in how they see. In the East, my work is attributed to Zen. In Scandinavia they see it according to their pure design aesthetics. Art unveils a hidden part of ourselves and revives the way we want to see the world. I think the silence in the work allows the viewer to exhale their inner world in the perceiving process.

Aaron: Do you have a particular ritual when working in your studio, whether straightforwardly religious or not?

Armen: I don't work; I either play or pray. I play until I come to something I believe in and can't stop pursuing obsessively. When you play or pray, you can't do either for someone else. You must play and pray for yourself. I believe that all art is playing seriously.

14. Barbara Takenaga: Chasing Cosmic Waves

Barbara Takenaga was born in North Platte, Nebraska and lives and works in New York City. She was the Mary A. and William Wirt Warren Professor of Art at Williams College, a position she held from 1985 to 2018. Her work has been widely exhibited at institutions including MASS MoCA and the Museum of Contemporary Art in Denver, Colorado, and she has designed public works for the New York MTA and NYU Langone. She was awarded a John Simon Guggenheim Fellowship in the field of fine arts in 2020. Her stunningly detailed abstract compositions suggest both cosmic and cellular forms.

Aaron: Do you have any ritual as part of your practice, either before you begin working or as you paint?

Barbara: Unfortunately not—no yoga warm-ups or mind-clearing exercises. I rarely make preliminary drawings, except an occasional doodle. Because the process begins with random pours of paint in a kind of faux abstract expressionist process—tipping the canvas, flinging paint, all of those historical dance moves—the image is determined by how the paint dries. I guess that could be the ritual, actually.

Aaron: Your paintings often seem to have a cosmic force whirling, flowing, or bursting through them (Figure 14.1). Is that there from the start, or does it pick up momentum as you paint?

Barbara: I like that description. In some ways, it's the nature of the paint itself, without me doing much to encourage the outcome. Liquid paint tends to pool or drag as it dries. It's a wonderful micro view of bigger forces—gravity, momentum, natural patterning. When I start working with brushes, I often just follow the direction of the paint in a kind of collaboration. But I must have a pull toward that kind of cosmic imagery, because it keeps emerging.

FIGURE 14.1

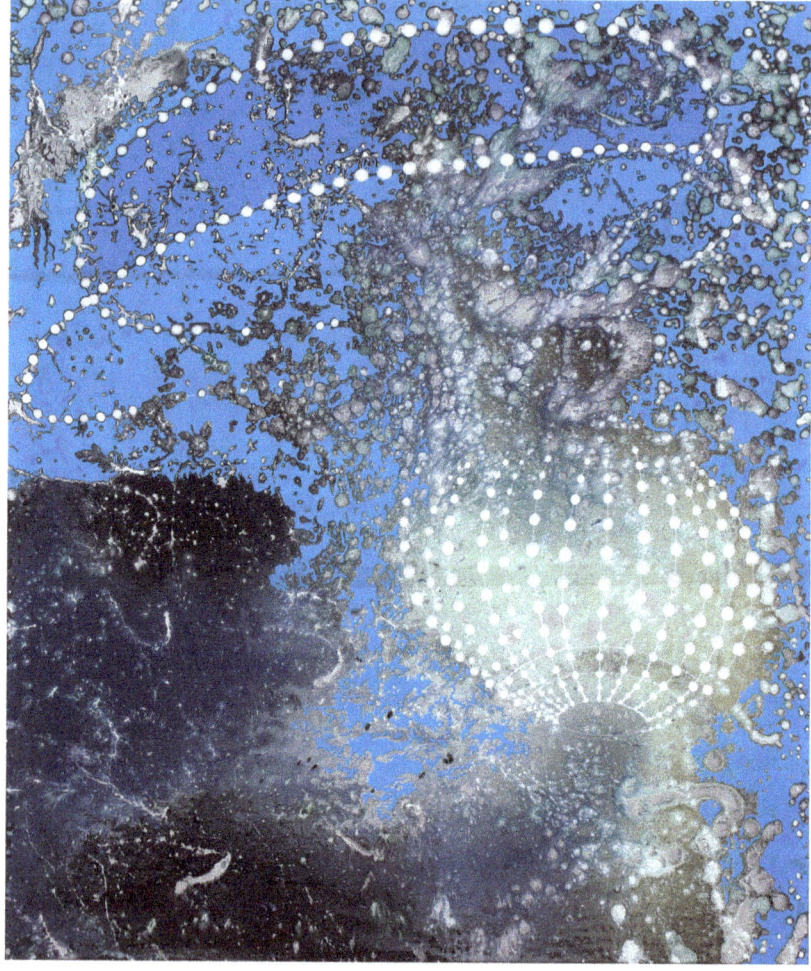

Aaron: What forms have you created on canvas that have most surprised you?

Barbara: Although I'm a bit of a control freak, I want to incorporate more randomness. So I often have to problem-solve images that are outside my comfort zone. Sometimes the underlying image is so blatant and awkward that I just have to give in and go with it. Those difficult ones, the ones that I have to wrestle with, are often the most surprising and rewarding.

FIGURE 14.2

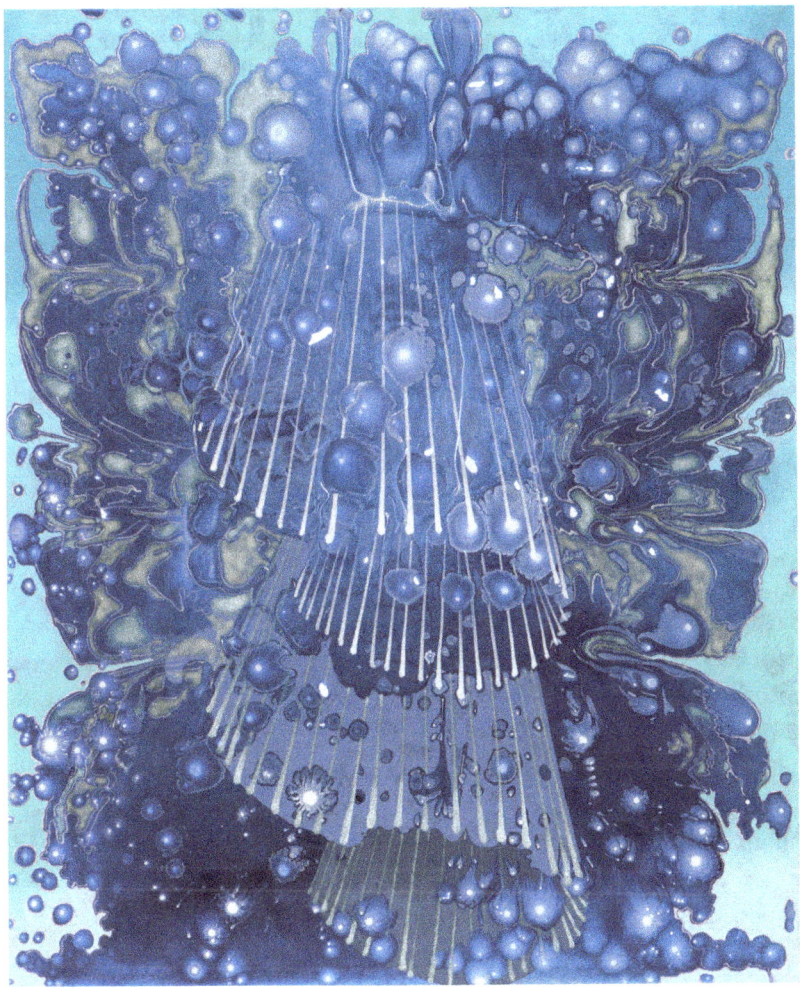

Aaron: Some of your works remind me of the heavenly patterns in the ceilings of religious spaces from the Dome of the Rock to Saint Peter's Basilica. If you could imagine your works filling a vast space, whether a ceiling or a wall, where would that be and what might it look like?

Barbara: That's a lovely idea and a really difficult question. Religious spaces have such beauty and presence, from the intention of the architecture, but also from usage. Who wouldn't love to have an immersive, monumental work in such a contemplative space? Ceiling *and* wall! It's an egomaniac's desire, impossibly alluring.

Aaron: There are a lot of ways to look at your works, not just interpretatively but visually. One could begin at the center or the perimeter, for example, or look into their space or dwell on their surface. Do you imagine viewers looking in a certain way when you paint? Have you learned any optic strategies from your viewers over the years?

Barbara: This question is actually at the center of the work. I like the idea of possibility—that the painting can carry multiple readings. It's like standing in the middle, at a still point, the old idea of reconciliation of opposites. I like to think of "visual tolerance": An image can be a cloud or a spaceship or a giant head. Missiles or falling stars (Figure 14.2). Cells or galaxies or bullet holes. I also started using iridescent paint. I love how it changes color with different kinds of light—it's a different image in the morning than in the evening. Or the color shifts as the viewer moves position. The painting has a little life of its own. It interacts and is not static.

Aaron: How have the strange events of this year impacted your work, whether explicitly or more subtly?

Barbara: 2020 has been a bounty of horrors. But I know that for a lot of artists, the quarantine meant hunkering down in the studio with not much else to do but work and wash our groceries and sanitize our keys. That was a small upside, all that concentrated studio time. No doubt the events of this year—pandemic, awful, divisive politics, wildfires, climate change, the beloved RBG leaving this world, as well as the examination of racism in our culture brought on by the Black Lives Matter movement—have had a big impact on my work. How could they not? But I'm still in the midst of it and myopic. I'm hoping 2021 is, as my father would say, more better.

Intimate Space

15. Anne Mourier:
The Quiet Power of a Gentle Gaze

Anne Mourier started training as an artist when she was a girl by taking care of others in the confinement of home. Then she took care of three children for twenty years. Her work is rooted in taking care and the home is her palette as she seeks to remind the world of the beauty and power of the feminine. She is a co-founder of the Invisible Dog in Brooklyn, New York and has exhibited across the United States and Europe. She divides her time between New York and Venice.

Aaron: I was walking on the beach today and I saw some shells that reminded me of things that might capture your attention. For those less familiar with your work, how might you define your aesthetic?

Anne: My work is really about my ongoing research into what the feminine is, how it's represented, and how we feel it in the world. It's not for me a question of gender—perhaps that's why a shell on the beach can remind you of my work—because I'm not talking about men and women. I'm talking about the feminine that is in all of us, the feminine that is in nature. I'm talking about the feminine so people remember how beautiful it is in a society that feels patriarchal, in which the masculine takes so much space. My idea is to help rebalance this a bit.

Aaron: I like how you insist that your work isn't really about gender or sex *per se*, but something that's at once almost mystical as well as tactile.

You use the feminine in such a fluid way. This seems so consistent over the course of your career, but have you seen people respond to that differently over time?

Anne: I feel people are getting a better understanding of what I'm doing, maybe partly because I express it in a way that's more understandable for people. I remember ten or twenty years ago, hearing things like "oh, your work is too girlie for me." I feel like men receive my work better than they used to. I decided early on that I really wanted to use the tools that represent my message. So often the work is small, understated, delicate. I remember years ago I was working with miniatures and a gallery said it was hard to show the work because it's so small. So I started making larger photographs of small objects, but still with a gentle voice.

Aaron: I think that's revealing. There's often this sense that scale is somehow correlative to artistic ambition. To me, your preference for things that are small is also echoed in your preference for private rather than public subjects. You bring us back as viewers to this quiet art of noticing and looking. Was this contemplative character there in your work from the beginning?

Anne: Yes. I developed the palette of colors that I'm still using today very, very early on in my photography . . . intimate . . . pastel colors. The sense of scale was there early too, in my small boxes, which are only three by six inches each (Figure 15.1). The other element that was there from the beginning was that feminine way of expressing things that can be delicate, sensitive. I'm trying to generate strong emotions in people that look at my work, to show them strength in a different way.

Aaron: That's very interesting in terms of how I might place you within the canon of art. Unlike, for example, the grand works of Judy Chicago, you don't rely on extroverted visual statements or manifestos to prove the power of the feminine.

I love these little boxes, which feel almost like frames in a graphic novel. Together, there's a narrative sensibility, not a sense of time that marches teleologically but one that's cyclical, defined by daily rhythms and tasks. I also love the hands descending from the sky, which reminds me of illuminated manuscripts where God's hands reach down from the clouds. Was it part of your thinking when you made these works that there's a divine feminine power animating these scenes?

Anne: It was not part of my thinking at the time, but now when you say it, it's very interesting. It began out of research into my own relationship with my mother. I'm originally from France, and in French "clean" and "proper" are the same word. I grew up in a family where all the women were absolutely obsessed with the idea of domesticity and purity. Keeping the house clean was the number one priority, even over taking care of your children's emotions. So the fact that there is no head, only arms in the boxes, is related to this obsession.

As for Judy Chicago, this is interesting. I can relate to a piece like the *Dinner Party*, for example, where the vulva is very present, as it is in my work, but I don't relate to the form that her expression takes: the giant size of the piece, the sharp edges of the triangle, the loud colors. All of that belongs to the masculine way of expressing ourselves, even if I recognize that at the time it was probably the only way for a feminist message to be heard. Even today I am taking the risk of not being heard or seen . . . and that's okay.

Aaron: Do you see a strong difference in rhetoric around domesticity between France, where you grew up, and the United States or Italy where you divide your time now?

FIGURE 15.1

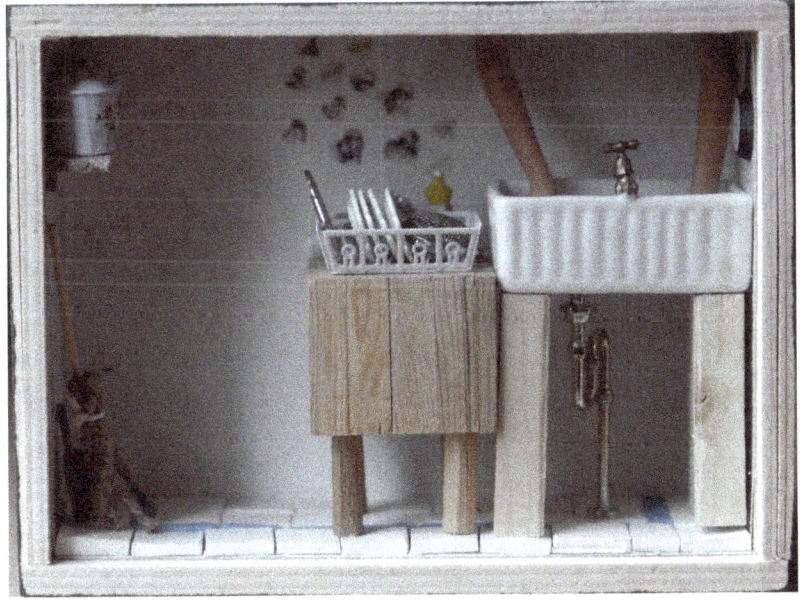

Anne: I think this is something that was definitely more prominent in Europe, especially in my mother's generation. But my first solo show was in Brooklyn, New York and was called *Cleaning It Up* and I met a lot of the visitors, especially older women, who could definitely relate to my experience. This is something that is definitely evolving.

Aaron: It'll be interesting to see how this evolves with Gen Z's take on domesticity, especially with the opening up of the private sphere into the public via social media, and trends like the #tradwife lifestyle propagated by conservative female influencers, trading on gender norm nostalgia. Switching gears, though, can you talk a bit about how you select the medium for your works?

Anne: To me the medium is just a way to express things. I love collaboration with people, which is very much part of the feminine archetype also. I love collaborating with highly skilled artisans. When I start envisioning a piece, usually early on I can also envision the best medium to do it in. But sometimes that changes. For example, I made some pieces as sculpture that ended up being photographs of the sculptures. And some pieces remain only as performances. For me the two most important parts of creating an artwork are the message and the aesthetics, not the medium.

FIGURE 15.2

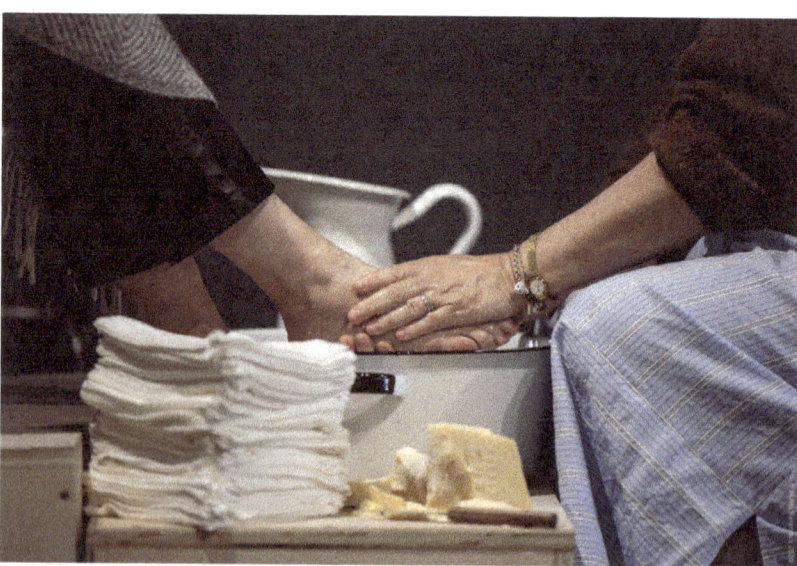

Aaron: I've had the opportunity to participate in one of those pieces, where you wash the feet of exhibition visitors (Figure 15.2). There's a reference to Mary of Bethany washing and perfuming Jesus' feet, and later his washing of the disciples' feet, which gives rise to the ritual of foot washing on Maundy Thursday. But there's also the art historical piece. I think of Mierle Laderman Ukeles' "maintenance art" performances, which seem to resist patriarchal values (and valuations) of art.

Thinking about cleaning, your broom pieces come to mind. Their gargantuan scale suggests "domestic goddesses" or witches. I'm interested in how you ended up exploring broom-making. You seem to have a gift for finding creative partners when you travel. How does this happen?

Anne: Well, the story with the brooms is typical of the way it happens. I was on my first residency in Maine a few years ago and I was looking for a good lobster roll in the middle of the winter. I pulled the car over and the lunch shop was closed, so I popped my head into this quiet little shop next door where Eric McInthyre was carving brooms and spoons. I can sense when someone is doing something with a sort of feminine quality. I just knocked on the door and started chatting with Eric, who told me that he had quit a job that was not fulfilling for him and was learning to do this carving. There was something extremely gentle and soft, with a lot of humility, in the way he presented what he was doing, and so I thought we could work together! The brooms of course relate to both: domesticity and witches.

Aaron: Would you call it a spiritual quality that you saw in his practice?

Anne: It's a connection that is extremely subtle. It's hard to describe, it's a feeling that someone deals with the world in the same way that I do. And again, it's about the feminine, not about gender. It's definitely not something rational.

Another example is the glass master I work with in Murano, Italy. He's nearly sixty years old, and he started when he was nine years old. It took him about twenty-five years to learn his craft. I come to the glass factory with sketches and then we discuss. My friend explained that Murano glass is actually alive—the molecules never stop moving in the glass. I wanted to create a piece about time moving in a circular way, a sense of sacred feminine time.

I asked my friend to create a dead rose out of living glass. But for the first time he didn't seem to quite understand the form I wanted. So at lunchtime we go out, and he said, "Okay, let me smoke a cigarette and understand. Tell me again what your concept is with this. What are you trying to say?" So I explained to him again, and he said, "Oh, I know. I didn't even listen because I have made millions of roses out of glass in my life, but I was always asked to make happy roses." So then we went back and created the fading rose I was looking for.

Aaron: I really like this way of being in the world, where you grapple through a vision together in order to translate it into form. It also gives an insight into how artists perceive things, where you both discover together the very subtle—to some probably invisible—difference between a rose which looks alive and vital and one that expresses a sense of loss and gravity.

Thinking of glass works like this, Amy Rahn, who curated your recent exhibition, has spoken about the level of faith you place in viewers. As she put it, "Your impulse was always to share it with the public above protecting it, and to trust the public to make the work a little vulnerable." Does that still come with certain trepidation for you?

Anne: I'm a mother, and to me the artworks are a little bit like babies. With my children, I wanted to dedicate a lot of time and care into having them grow up, but once they were ready to go into the world, I wanted complete freedom for them—both roots and wings—and it's a little similar with my work. I take a lot of care making a piece, but once it's ready and it's out in the world, whatever happens to it is just what's supposed to happen. It's happened a couple of times that pieces got broken, and sometimes they even got better, whether I fix them or use the pieces some other way. I really trust this process. I feel like I'm guided by something outside of me. The most important thing, the reason why I'm doing this work, is to share ideas and emotions.

Aaron: That's a powerful analogy. I can't say I have quite that much faith, either as a parent or as a writer and curator. Perhaps my (somewhat less trusting) version would be that the only way to teach the world to handle beautiful, breakable things is by giving them to it nonetheless, in spite of all we know of the world.

Anne: To me, the exchange with human beings, the emotions that we share in front of a piece of artwork, is something of much more value than the material object by itself. So I think it's part of the message, too. And even in breakage, there might be knowledge produced.

Aaron: Does that mean we should expect even more fragile works in the future?

Anne: Actually, I made a big decision for my work recently. I decided that I don't think I want to keep making new objects. It feels like where we are with the environment that adding objects to the world is not necessary. At least that's the way it feels to me. What I love is the connection with people, [so] I would like to do more intangible pieces like performances and happenings. Maybe these could be big, strong, and very gentle at the same time.

16. Cate Pasquarelli: America the Uncanny

Cate Pasquarelli received a BFA from the Cooper Union. Her work is included in the collections of Beth Rudin DeWoody as well as Jim Jarmusch and Sara Driver. She was recently awarded a programming fellowship at the Wassaic Project and her work has been exhibited at SPRING/BREAK in New York and Los Angeles.

Aaron: You seem to find elements of pastoral American life beguiling—school buses, steepled churches, picket fences. Where does that fascination come from?

Cate: There's a kind of anonymity to those things that still somehow feels decidedly American. Books and movies paint these pastoral pictures over and over in a way that makes them feel like the language of generic American life. Maybe it's because I grew up in a city that they seem fascinating. To me there's something alluring about rural life simply because I've never lived it. I think we're all naturally intrigued by—and maybe a little suspicious of—the worlds that are unfamiliar to us.

Aaron: We've spoken about your interest in American literature, especially modern and contemporary short stories set in small towns. I'm curious what writers and themes are especially generative for your work.

Cate: I love stories that make ordinary things feel strange and strange things feel ordinary. Small towns are the perfect setting for this sort of thing. Two of my favorite writers, Shirley Jackson and Flannery O'Connor, were writing during the political and cultural turbulence of the 1950s and sixties through a sort of surreal lens. They focus on rural white America, with characters who cling to traditional values to feed their racist agendas. Both writers use whimsical elements, but their stories usually end in horrifying ways—like a woman being stoned to death by her family and neighbors or a grandmother getting shot in the road. They explore relationships between skeptics and believers, young people and old people, locals and "strangers."

Aaron: Why do you think the mythology of rural America has such a pull on the American imagination?

Cate: When something happens in a town where nothing happens, an entire community is turned upside down. I think that's why myths, stories, and secrets are held more tightly in small towns than in cities, where people can hide behind their anonymity. In rural areas, neighbors know each other like their grandparents knew each other, and there is a sense of trust that can't exist in a more populated area. It's the perfect breeding ground for misinformation, rumors, corruption, and cults. If you are an artist or a writer, a small town is a great place to set the scene for something entirely deranged.

FIGURE 16.1

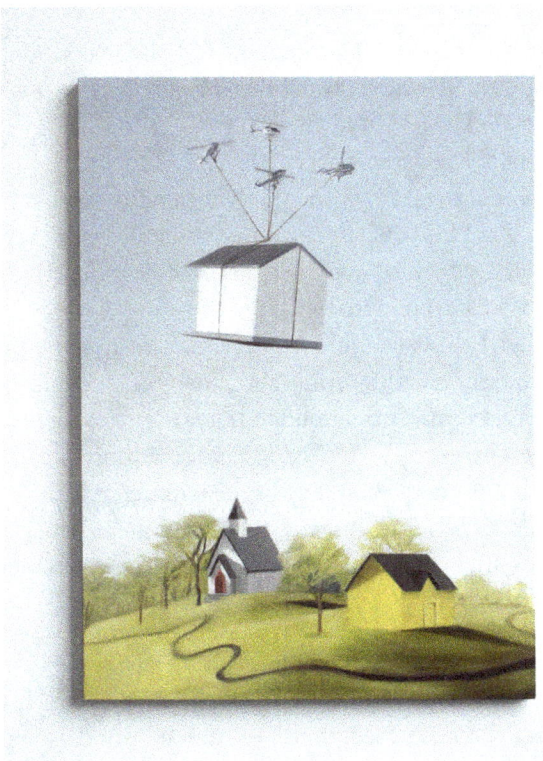

Aaron: Classic New England church buildings crop up often in your work (Figure 16.1), sometimes as part of the scenery, but at other times more as characters unto themselves. While the forms are of course drawn from a particular Christian vernacular, do they have further spiritual significance to you?

Cate: Personally, the churches don't hold a lot of spiritual meaning to me, as I don't have much of a relationship to Christianity now. But they do hold significant symbolic meaning to me when I consider what fascinates me about small New England towns and what hides behind their white picket fences and smiling neighbors.

Each building in a town holds its own stories, conversations, and secrets. In a way, they feel much more like portraits of the people who have lived there than features of a landscape. The church motif comes up a lot in my work simply because churches are such a prevalent part of colonial architecture and our country's darkest histories.

Aaron: What was your own experience of religion like growing up?

Cate: My brother and I went to a progressive Episcopal school in Lower Manhattan where we attended chapel three times a week. By the time I was in middle school, I wondered why I was the only kid in my class not to receive communion. My parents asked a friend of theirs who was a priest to sit down with me and talk it over. They decided it was okay for me to participate as long as I knew what it meant. As a family, we never identified with any particular religion. My parents had different beliefs, and I think they wanted us to make our own decisions.

Three years ago, I returned to the same school as a teacher, and it all felt very strange to me. For one thing, only about half the students participated in chapel. I had a hard time explaining to them why they were required to be there, or why it wasn't okay to play tic-tac-toe during the service. I still have trouble with it. I worry about how some children might feel confused or alienated by the experience. It seems to me that inclusivity is more than inviting people of different faiths to join your service. It's also about giving them the space to opt out.

Aaron: The great sociologist of religion Peter Berger spoke of religion as providing a "sacred canopy" for believers in moments of existential uncertainty. You seem to paint and sculpt little enchanted worlds, then pull away the canopy by introducing a disaster that disturbs the bucolic scene. Do you imagine the inhabitants of your scenes facing crises of meaning?

Cate: That's precisely it. I think of the inhabitants as people who have managed to self-isolate for a long time and whose lives are suddenly disrupted by immense change. In this moment of crisis, some are willfully blind to disaster, while others actively push against what is unfamiliar, driving them to extreme circumstances in either case. That inner turmoil is visible in the imprint they leave on the landscape.

I often think about a story by Flannery O'Connor titled "The River." A little boy's babysitter brings him to a river where a revivalist preacher baptizes the boy and explains that he is loved by his heavenly father, the Lord. The boy returns home to his parents, who struggle with alcoholism and generally ignore him. In search of his other dad in the kingdom of heaven, the boy goes back to the river and drowns in the current. I think many of us are that little boy. We're just looking for some kind of love and meaning in the world. It's easy not to notice when it's killing us.

Aaron: Another way to look at your works, especially given their glass enclosures, is that they simulate specimens in a natural history museum or dioramas in an ethnographic museum. Do you think of your works as collecting or preserving a certain type of world?

Cate: I wouldn't go so far as to say that they capture a historically accurate picture of the world we're living in. I'm telling the story of a kind of rural life I've never lived. But they do capture something real about the way that life appears from the outside, the way it feels.

In my last show, I created a "Museum of Embellished History" to contextualize my landscapes in a made-up town I called New Bantam. The imagery was surreal, like a plume of smoke that travels between two chimneys (Figure 16.2), or a government building being airlifted by helicopters out of a hamlet (Figure 16.1). I created a fictional artist for the works, Peter Landon, whose picture hung on a wall—a photograph of me with a mustache. Still, because I called it a museum and had a bit of wall text that told a vague story, surprisingly to me, many people believed these events had really occurred. They asked me questions like "What year was this?" and "Where is New Bantam located?"

It's interesting to me how quick we are to trust a museum's account of history simply because it's presented in a way that feels organized and professional. We gloss over whatever seems unappealing or doesn't fit into the story we are trying to tell. In many ways, I think fiction can tell a more honest story than what we consider to be the truth.

FIGURE 16.2

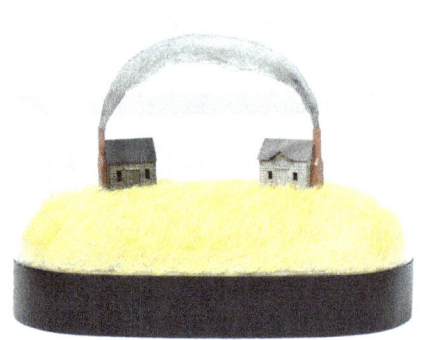

Aaron: In an era of catastrophic climate change, the disasters you allude to seem both archetypal—like a biblical deluge—and also highly specific, reminding me of the recent floods in Vermont, for example. Would it be fair to think of your recent work as a form of witness?

Cate: Strangely enough, I started working on a sculpture called *Flood* before the Vermont floods. What was supposed to be kind of a surreal, dramatic image now feels eerily prophetic. That overlap between dream worlds and reality interests me. I don't even need to stretch the truth very far to make a point. The world is a strange, perverted place, and we're living in enough of a nightmare as it is.

17. Kylee Snow: Good Bones

Kylee Snow is a figurative artist working primarily in graphite. Her current body of work takes inspiration from old New England homes, exploring the deep relationships between home and inhabitants. Originally from Vermont, she is based in Brooklyn and completed her MFA at the New York Academy of Art.

Aaron: What is it about graphite that compels you?

Kylee: I love graphite's simplicity and reflectivity. People often minimize its reflective quality, but I love how dramatically it interacts with light, so that a piece never looks the same. Graphite also mirrors a narrative ambiguity I try to bring to the work. The effort to grasp the image ties to the effort to grasp its meaning. Graphite's lack of material complexity also feels honest. Since it's a simple form of carbon, any mystery in a graphite work is created through process, and that feels like starting from a place of truth.

Aaron: People often think of drawing as a preparatory process rather than a culmination in itself. How do you play with or subvert that expectation?

Kylee: I've been drawing since childhood, and years ago I decided I would go as deep into details as I could, like I was a microscope. It was fascinating to realize there is always more texture and value, and to learn to connect the detail to the full narrative. While I have moved toward combining direct observation with more imagined elements, I find that my self-taught and somewhat obsessive practice of deep noticing remains an undercurrent in my work. I like to know as much as I can about one specific thing. There's power in continually realizing that there is always more to learn. I enjoy pushing a medium often used simply into a more complicated space.

Aaron: Paul Gauguin wrote in his diaries that his drawings contained his secrets. I think of that when looking at many of your works. Is the sense of secrecy or hiddenness important in your work?

FIGURE 17.1

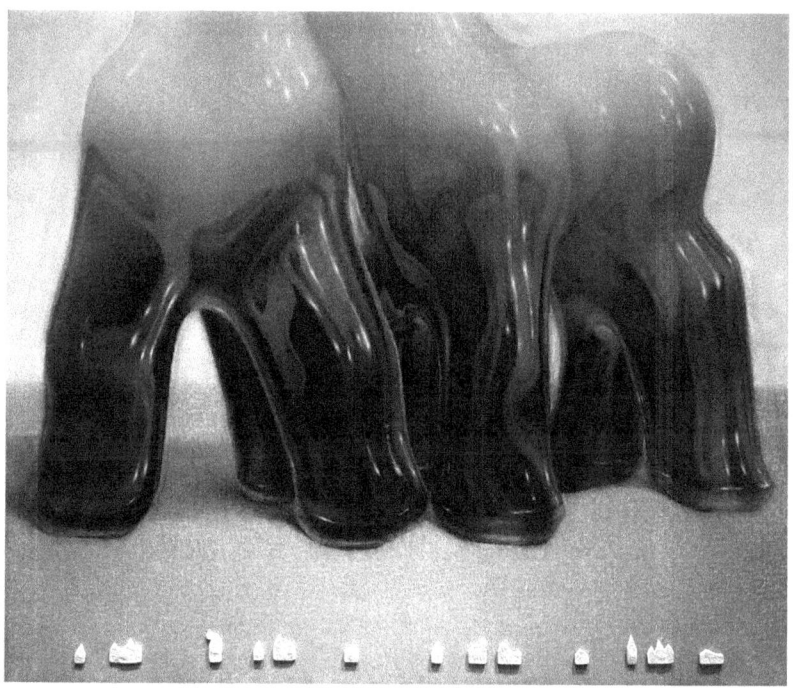

Kylee: I'm currently exploring how we live in communication with built space, specifically the homes we know intimately (Figure 17.1). I'm interested in how we interact with and transform our homes to be ours and how that built space forms us in return. I'm also thinking about the home as a being itself, how it envelops the accumulation of small changes over time and lives on its own timeline as inhabitants pass through it. My recent work all takes place in and around the same imagined home. I feel like I'm building it and its history piece by piece. The work encompasses my own secrets when I pull details from my homes and possessions, and the unknown secrets of others when I find inspiration from historical homes and objects.

As I think about our complex relationships with our spaces, I've been envisioning bones as a static symbol of a life. Every bone is the remainder of a being and contains a lifetime of secrets. I keep thinking of the phrase "good bones" in relation to parallels between homes and our own bodies. Bones are our inner structure, supporting us as we make our homes our own and live within their built skeletons. Each skeletal system supports the other, and both contain multitudes of secrets.

Aaron: Another strong feeling I get when I spend time with your work is uncanniness. How do you evoke the uncanny without just getting straight-forwardly spooky?

Kylee: I am always trying to walk a line between telling too much and too little. Spooky is obvious and overt, built on clear and recognizable cultural symbols and evoking specific feelings. Uncanny is sneaky—using and sub-verting symbols to evoke feelings that are harder to define. I have my own thoughts, stories, and feelings that go into the work, but I never want those to be obvious. I want to connect to something universal through subjects that elicit others' feelings and draw on their personal histories and secrets. Graphite is quiet, and I try to be subtle but with some underlying, often uncanny disquiet.

Aaron: Are there specific places and histories you've used for inspiration, or do you work more from the imagination?

Kylee: I have a long ancestral history in New England and strong ties to the home in Vermont where I grew up. The imagined home I am constructing is an amalgamation of historical New England homes, personal and famil-ial histories, and imagined content and compositions. I am also inspired by literature and currently thinking a lot about Gaston Bachelard's *The Poetics of Space*.

Aaron: Many of your works involve "ghost images," conjuring a palimpsest in which previous images seem to hover and evade full erasure. How do you achieve this effect technically, and what does it signify to you?

Kylee: As I've been focusing on relationships with physical homes, I've also been thinking a lot about perceptions of time. We all exist within the rules of this extremely personal, indescribable thing that makes everything what it is and dictates everything we know and experience. Everything we in-teract with has its own timeline, separate from but intersecting with ours, and on some level must have its own perception of time. The palimpsest is a strategy to explore how an old home might experience time. For example,

I built *Organic Habits* (Figure 17.2) from imagination, beginning with the solid, immovable physicality of the house itself, then adding furniture and decoration, overlapping and changing, then finally traces of people, envisioned as patterns in which the home might guide them over time.

FIGURE 17.2

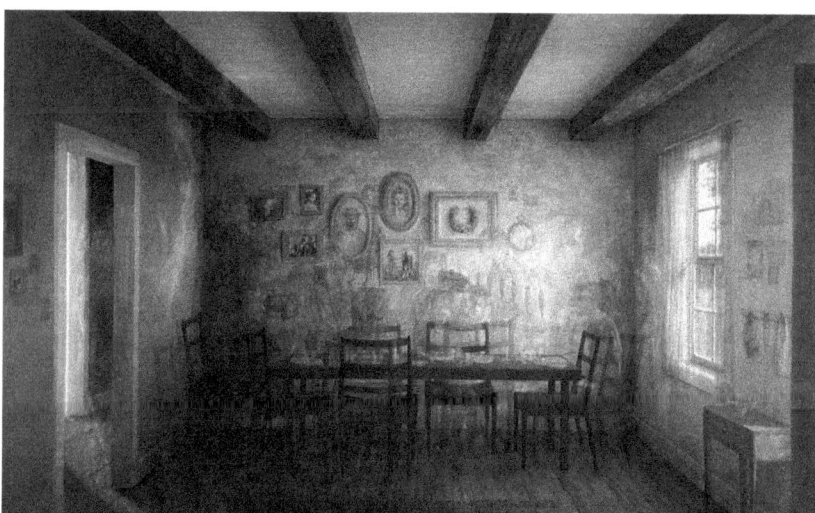

Aaron: Recently you seem to be homing in on specific objects more than scenes. Do you think of these objects as bearing an aura or a sense of the sacred?

Kylee: Objects can have deep known or unknown histories. They interact with the homes they occupy and hold meaning for each person they belong to. I like to think that, like bones, they can carry hidden memories, connections, and secrets in their materiality. I think of these household objects as bearing their own auras accumulated over years of use. They live with and beyond us in a complicated web of movement and time, bearing witness to and participating in life.

18. Sobia Ahmad: Here Is a Ritual

Sobia Ahmad is a Pakistani-American interdisciplinary artist with a background in public health. Her practice explores the transcendental power of everyday experiences, objects, and rituals through photography, time-based media, and social practice. She holds an MFA from the Carnegie Mellon University School of Art.

Aaron: Can you talk a bit about your background and how you grew up?

Sobia: I was born and raised in Pakistan in a multigenerational household. I come from a lineage of farmers on both sides, and our shared ways of being were and are rooted in that modest way of living. My childhood was filled with large family gatherings and shared meals. Eid celebration days especially were about food, punctuated with five collective prayers. We'd lay out blankets and prayer rugs in the courtyard, and all the aunts, uncles, grandmas, and cousins would stand shoulder to shoulder to perform *salat*, the Islamic prayer. I really value that prayer, both in the house and at the mosque, was a huge part of my childhood. I moved to the US when I was fourteen and went straight to high school. It was quite a transition!

Aaron: How have ideas of diaspora and home surfaced in your work?

Sobia: I'm interested in how immigrant, uprooted, and exiled communities create sanctuaries through spiritual practices, ancestral rituals, and inherited memories. In my practice, I explore the notion of home from various angles—physical, geographical, spiritual—to break open what a home is and can be.

In my recent work, I've explored how sociopolitical power structures affect our understanding of home. But I am not interested in limiting ways of belonging, and home to me is not a country or a nationality. It's both bigger and smaller than that. I do have an attachment to the courtyard of my childhood home. It resurfaces in my dream-memory a lot, and I think of it as a container for ancestral knowledge.

Aaron: Recently, you've been learning a lot of new skills connected to your family and heritage. Can you talk about that process and what it's unlocking for you?

Sobia: I've become interested in various craft and weaving techniques and am attempting to re-create everyday objects that were part of my childhood. I'm currently working on a traditional woven bed of the kind that served multiple purposes in the courtyard of my home—a daybed, a surface to clean rice or dry chilis on, a gathering place (Figure 18.1).

FIGURE 18.1

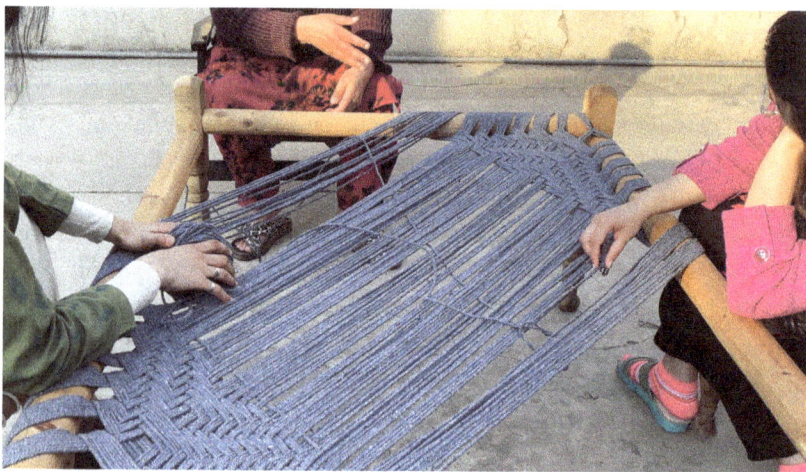

I'm crowdsourcing these skills from local weavers and the older women in my family who are now scattered all over the world. They're sharing stories of various such beds they'd woven or inherited and sending videos and patterns, all of which I'm organizing into a knowledge bank of sorts. It feels like I'm gathering pieces of a puzzle from different loved ones. It's a multigenerational effort that is shifting my studio practice in magical ways.

The craft and materiality of weaving is not only helping me to reconnect with family history but also bringing me back into my own body. I didn't know I was yearning to work with my hands so much. It's a very slow process, and I'm really enjoying being a beginner. I'm thinking of it as an exercise in both "wrest" and rest. I am not only learning to slow down, but I'm also unlearning a lot, especially my constant participation in the productivity culture that I had internalized so much.

Aaron: When you and I have spoken, the word *here* comes up a lot. What kind of temporal and spatial experience do you want viewers to have when they see your work?

Sobia: The idea of "here" became very present for me during the early months of the pandemic while I was living near Rock Creek Park in DC. During quarantine, I spent a lot of time among the trees. That daily solitary ritual of walking in the woods pushed me into a contemplative space that helped me navigate my own and our shared grief and joys in a grounding way.

"Here" can be anything: here is the pandemic; here is the long over-due reckoning with white supremacy; here can also be a momentary state of mind, an intimate inner struggle, or a physical location. What happens when our personal and collective heres intersect, intertwine, and collide? Our heres are ever shifting and may be marked by unease, yet being present to our heres can show us myriad possibilities (Figure 18.2).

FIGURE 18.2

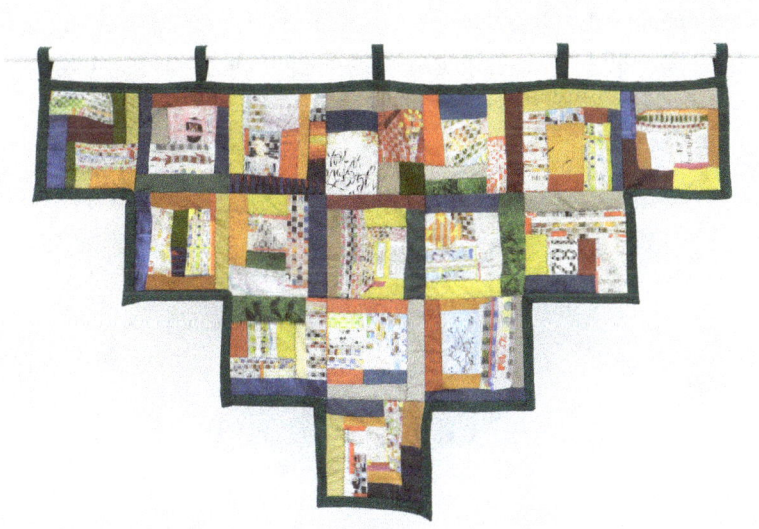

I've invited many people into this idea via workshops that reflect on the idea of here through a project called *Marking Here(s)*. Participants receive a mail packet containing simple craft materials, instructions on gathering materials for weaving, and a postcard with some poetic invitations for visual journaling and creating a simple ritual that they carry out for a week. A week later, we gather to meditate, share, and weave. I guide the participants through a series of creative exercises to mark their own idiosyncratic here(s) and gain a deeper awareness of our own internal landscapes and our various shared realities. Final weavings are shared with me via mail and transformed into an object relevant to the group that I worked with. Some of these final works have included a quilt, prayer flags, a zine, and an accordion book.

Aaron: Do you have particular ritual practices—religious or not—you find yourself returning to in the studio?

Sobia: I regularly listen to Qawwali in the studio. It helps me enter my flow state. Qawwali is the devotional music of Sufis from Pakistan and India. It's mystical poetry by Sufi saints written hundred of years ago and sung by ensembles of folk singers from the region. I also listen to the podcast *On Being* in the studio. My favorite part is Krista Tippett's opening question to each guest: "Was there a religious or spiritual background to your childhood? How does it inform who you are now?" I love the multiplicity of ways people enter that question. Also, I recently put a prayer rug in the studio that's doubling as my nap corner. Napping is a new practice for me that I hope to continue.

Control and Surrender

19. Bernd Haussmann: Dark as Light

Bernd Haussmann divides his time between the Massachusetts coast and the Maine woods, where he and his wife, Anne, also work on a 450-acre nature project. His work is exhibited in national and international art fairs and is visible in numerous private, corporate, and museum collections around the world. His teachings revolve around mindfulness in and through art, encouraging environmental, inclusionary, interactive projects and collaborations.

Aaron: Recently, we collaborated on an exhibition of your work entitled *Dark Night Dark Light* at The Parsonage Gallery in Maine (Figure 19.1). For many readers, your exhibition title will evoke thoughts of the Catholic mystic St. John of the Cross and his "Dark Night of the Soul." What kinds of theological ideas did you have in mind when you were preparing the exhibition?

Bernd: *Dark Night* speaks of the source, *Dark Light* of change and the natural rhythm of all existence. This is what I had in mind for our show, an idea that I had presented in a somewhat different form in Tübingen, Germany, in 2022.

Dark Night Dark Light evokes many notions, ideas, and emotions that evolved naturally from my practice of art-making. I am not interested in any particular idea, concept, or school of contemplation or practice. But it is my intention to stay open to all. I am interested in learning through my practice. In Buddhism and the Advaita Vedanta this is called direct experiencing, infinite open awareness, big mind.

FIGURE 19.1

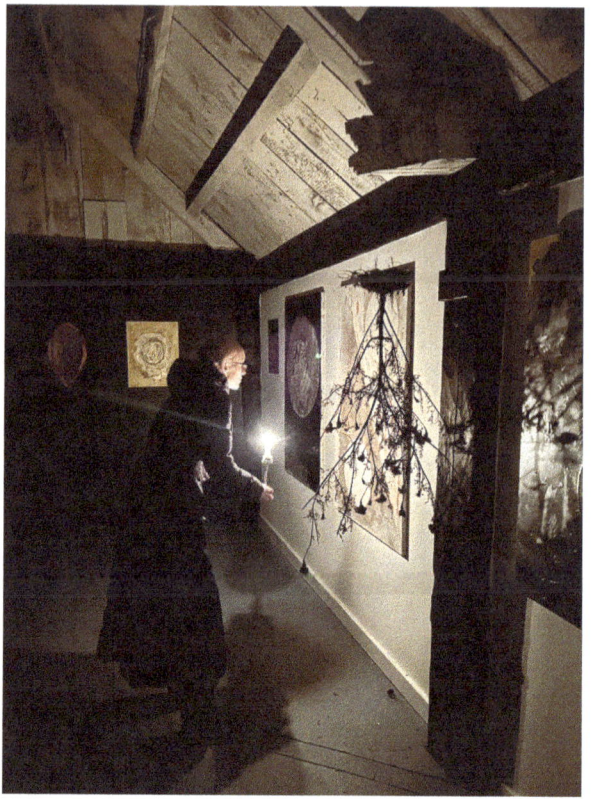

Drawing from the source directly is the practice that I call ART. When I speak of ART I mean it in a holistic, direct experiential way. A stands for Awareness, R for Realization, T for Truth. ART is the overarching presence/awareness before and after all things. That substrate that people call consciousness.

The practice came first. The ideology second. In the beginning was the picture—and then came the word. In the end the word is only in the way of the practice. Unlearning, or rather cultivating beginner's mind, is one of the most crucial points of my practice. Philosophy, science, and several wisdom traditions enrich, expand, and give me confirmation by putting into words what I find in my practice. I am mostly interested in non-dualism or closely related explorations and practices.

Aaron: I'm interested in how you balance control and surrender in your practice. To pick one example, if you've created works in light, does exhibiting them in darkness change your relationship to them? Will they be shown in clear light in the future, or have they become creatures of darkness, as it were?

Bernd: There are many paintings that I created in total darkness in the past—in order to eliminate all visual distractions and to give up control—which were then later presented in light. The works in this exhibit were selected because I was curious how they would present themselves to the viewer under those specific conditions of darkness. They will return into the light and hopefully continue to speak in whichever environment they are placed in. In reality, any painting, at the studio, storage facility, gallery, public, or private space will live her life partly in darkness. They don't disappear, they are there even when we don't see them. Each painting responds in a unique way to her ever-changing environment. They emerged from darkness, the source darkness that I have talked about, and live in darkness and light until they return back to that original darkness, which I would call the big soup or consciousness. The unconditioned primal state.

I try to be passionately disengaged from my works and see no good reason to hold on to any of them. Once they have spoken to me, I trust that the truth they shared and reminded me of will remain in me.

Aaron: It seems to me that you're doing something rather unique by returning viewers to a more antiquated, mysterious experience, with parallels in candlelit cathedrals or even caves. How have you seen viewers react?

Bernd: There used to be a time when there was darkness and light. One could get up at 4:30 AM and sit outside and observe the gentle change from darkness to light. And in the evening the same thing, just in reverse. Like a slow and soft breath in and out, hardly noticeable, but very present when you are really awake. We sacrificed the night. And what is left of it we are scared of—what St. John of the Cross called the darkness of the soul.

There are two darknesses. The one I just mentioned, the scary one, and the one that is before dark and light. The darkness of the womb, the source, the god before GOD—consciousness, the non-dualistic view, the absolute, the one out of which dark and light emerge from and return to.

Because we lost the other side of light (meaning darkness) we also lost that original darkness, the spiritual one and the creative one. When dark and light are not in balance and in codependence of each other, and the one takes over, we not only play a devastatingly destructive game with the biology of nature, we also sacrifice the mystical, the spiritual, the unseeable, the unknowable, the metaphysical with the loss of our naturalness. That recognition is what I sensed some of the viewers experienced while exploring the space, creating their own pictures, finding their own way guided by the light they carried.

Aaron: Many of these works have natural elements embedded within them (Figure 19.2). Can you talk a bit more about that process, and how the environment around your Maine home shaped this body of work?

FIGURE 19.2

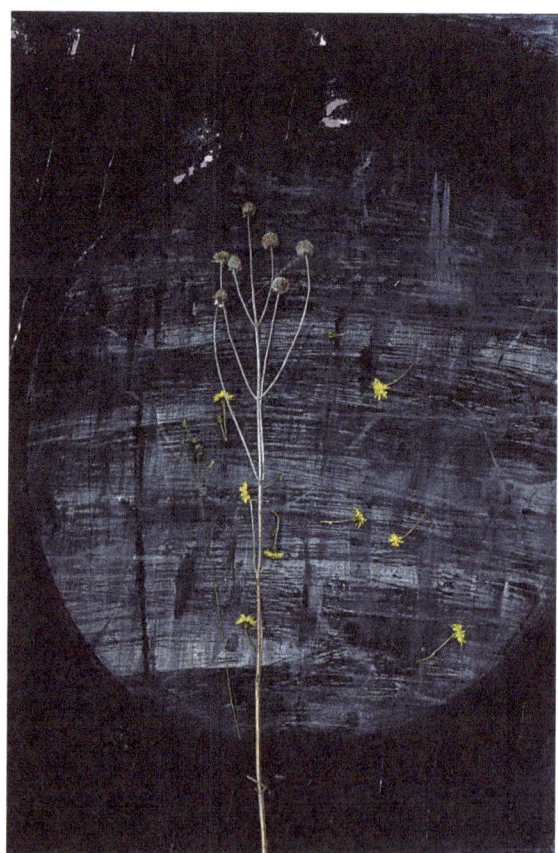

Bernd: I trust that ART is nature and nature is ART. Bringing elements into the picture from the natural world within which these works evolved seemed to be an obvious choice. There is so much to talk about but there is so much more to see. ART is a form of self-remembering, of self-realization, an opening for direct experiencing. As my wife and I live our ART, our surroundings in Maine are helpful in experiencing life, in not surrendering in these times of darkness. In ART, the big and overwhelmingly scary questions become smaller, more clear and approachable—sometimes even answerable—as we recognize the nature that we really are.

Aaron: When we opened this exhibition, it was only a few days after a mass shooting in Lewiston, Maine. We spoke about whether or not to postpone the exhibition, ultimately deciding to go ahead as planned. Can you explain why you felt so passionate about seeing art in that kind of moment?

Bernd: ART speaks most vividly and clearly in times of darkness. I think the only way to not surrender is to let the ART speak loud and clear especially in times of darkness. And speak of our true deep self and our intrinsic values. ART brings light into darkness. ART can show us the way.

> Often so many of us are lost, and so scared and confused that we turn away even from the natural light inside which could still guide us.
> Darkness carries the unknowable.
> Light carries knowledge.
> More light means more insight.
> May we all come to our senses.

Aaron: To me the soundtrack that played in the exhibition had its own rather liturgical feel, like vespers being sung in outer space. What is the music and how did you select it?

Bernd: The soundtrack is the "product" of me being the artist-in-residence at the Broad Institute of Harvard and MIT and a collaboration with Neil Leonard and his students at Berklee College of Music in Boston. The aim was to make audible the spectrum of life and its infinite flavors. This particular piece is called "Female Rabbit DNA" and was composed by Zoe Zai.

Music has always been with me as an active component of my practice, playing, and creating as a musician and a visual artist. An integral part of my being. So in the very beginning maybe there was music and then pictures and then words. At least that seems to fit my biography.

Many sound pieces have inspired this project, which really started maybe thirty years ago. I am moved by sources that speak of darkness and light, from Bach's last fugue to Mahler's "Urlicht" or Schumann's "Nachtlied." Music, like all ART and meditation, creates openings for direct experiencing. This is what I am after.

20. Devon DeJardin: Time to Gather Stones

Devon DeJardin (b. 1993) is a self-taught multimedia artist from Portland, Oregon currently based in Los Angeles. His paintings and sculptures of large guardian figures draw upon his study of spiritual traditions from around the world. DeJardin's work has been exhibited in galleries and fairs across the world.

FIGURE 20.1

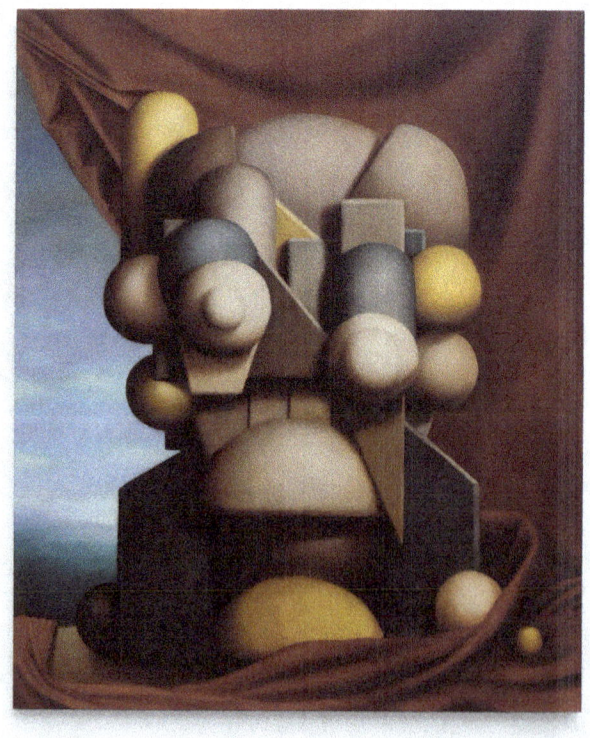

Aaron: The gallery we're speaking in (Albertz Benda Gallery, New York City) has the feeling of a sort of *sanctum sanctorum*. And right behind us is one of your large paintings with a veil in it (Figure 20.1), perhaps another nod to the ancient temple in Jerusalem. Playing with that idea, let's see if we can pull back the curtain on your practice a bit. Could you talk about how your spiritual journey has intersected with your artistic journey?

Devon: Well, my first creative work was actually in fashion, beginning from the time I was a teenager. It was going really well and I moved down to California to grow the business, but nothing sold. So I was based in Los Angeles with no money, bumming on my friend's couch.

And then I got this message from someone: "Can I pay you a hundred bucks to talk to you for ten minutes." And I thought, "Well, this is really interesting . . . I hope this doesn't turn into a crime investigation!" Anyways, I got on the phone with him and he asked me, "Hey, man, are you into religion, are you spiritual?" He didn't know that I'd actually studied world religions for years in university, reflecting on how can we tap into God through different perspectives. We started talking about this and he said, "I've been praying for you, and I really think you're supposed to start painting." In the moment, I just thought, "Oh, that's interesting, man. Thanks for the hundred bucks."

But six months after that phone call, I picked up my first canvas and was drawing on my friend's table and sharing some images. Then a couple months later, I made a kind of primitive resemblance of the figures you see now. A friend bought that piece, then his parents bought some work, and it started to feel like one of those divine moments, where you feel a voice saying, "You're supposed to start doing this."

Aaron: I can definitely see diverging paths that phone call could have taken! I'm interested in why you were receptive to that language of spiritual calling. And what happened between that moment when you heard "the call"—in a literal and spiritual sense—and when you decided to pick up a paintbrush?

Devon: Well, during that time studying comparative religion, I spent two and a half months in Israel, and then also in Haiti learning about Vodou (voodoo). I think I've always had this kind of yearning and willingness to learn from people, to listen to their experiences rather than rejecting them as crazy. It seems arrogant in a sense to talk about a divine moment, but I'm definitely open to receiving things in this way.

Aaron: That sense of being captivated by someone's gaze or voice seems to have a parallel in your work. They seem to look us in the eye with a sense of address. Is that how you envision your works speaking to people?

Devon: I try to push for a confrontational aspect to the work. The central points are the eyes, and they are actually the only shapes within my paintings that are never altered in color. They always remain a shade of white. They convey the idea of purity, of receiving something.

Aaron: That unchanging nature of the eye is intriguing. They're not lidded, and thus in a sense forever open. I'm reminded of the biblical image of scales falling from the eyes in a moment of revelation.

Devon: To me, the eyes are always central to understanding. And looking face-to-face there's the potential to surrender to something.

Aaron: We're surrounded by portrait-style images of your guardian figures. They could easily be arrayed in judgment, but there is an element of tranquility in their gaze.

Devon: For me, their identity as guardians comes from my studies of religion and different perspectives and worldviews. We all know that faiths are separate and unique, but what's the common thread between them? When we focus on separate ideologies, there just tends to be more turmoil, pain, and suffering. For me the thread that ties atheists, Christians, Buddhists, and others together is the desire to have a spiritual protector guiding you through this world, or into the next one—whether that's an animal, a person, or a deity. My figures offer this non-theological symbol of protection, regardless of what you believe. If this is placed in a home, you can feel that it's a protector watching over you, however you see that.

Aaron: I think it's refreshing that you're so willing to talk about religion in this way, and to delve into parallels between traditions. Could you talk a bit more about some of the inspiration you find in the protector forms in different traditions?

Devon: Well, sentinels appear in stacked stone forms created by arctic First Nations. They can be practical navigational tools, but also meditative in their construction. I like the idea that people would use stone forms to guide them from one location to the next. You knew you were on the right path if you found these structures, and I like this idea of a guiding force. I also think of pre-Islamic Arabian sculptures, and the use of found stones. When I came to the practice of painting, I really wanted to use fundamental shapes or building blocks to tell a story. You could say that the entire universe is really created from shapes, and I think there's a spiritual dimension that comes from the concept of form.

Aaron: In a sense, your way into painting was to gather stones. Very Ecclesiastes! It's hard to say whether you were creating shapes, or indeed finding them, letting the medium reveal them to you. It's also interesting that as you located these forms on canvas they started to combine in ways that signaled human presence. There are some theorists that postulate that religion itself originated out of our predisposition to find meaningful human presence in the world around us, from a shape on the horizon to a rock or tree in front of us, and that we then began to attribute powers to those forms.

Devon: With a semicircle mouth structure and two eyes, that's all you really need to create a human-like presence, even though the other elements are completely abstract. People often ask if my figures are humans, and I say: they could be, but they don't have to be.

Aaron: You've mentioned that you like to leave something in each series that beckons or points to a future series. I wonder if your painting of forms facing one another in this show suggests a growing interest in these guardians as part of some *sacra conversazione* (Figure 20.2). Do you see your sentinels forming some sort of community?

Devon: They can also be a reflection of yourself. Or myself. There can be a sense of journey, whether of control or surrender.

Aaron: Thinking more about this inward experience, can you describe what your studio practice is like? I'm fond of something Philip Guston once said, possibly derived from John Cage: at the start of a studio session there are all sorts of people present in your mind, and then one by one everyone leaves. And, if you're really lucky, even yourself.[1] Do you identify with that feeling of surrender?

Devon: Yeah, it's a constant battle in the studio between control and surrender. So much of my life in the past was about controlling every aspect or

1. Mayer, "My Father, Philip Guston," 24.

situation. In the studio, so much of the process you do control by mixing the paints, having your maquettes, doing your lighting, etc. But the moment you start painting you have to surrender to the fact that it's probably never going to go as you intend. And then you have that moment of surrender, this understanding that this painting can be more life-driven than you could ever imagine. I feel like I just have to surrender more and more every single day.

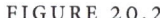

FIGURE 20.2

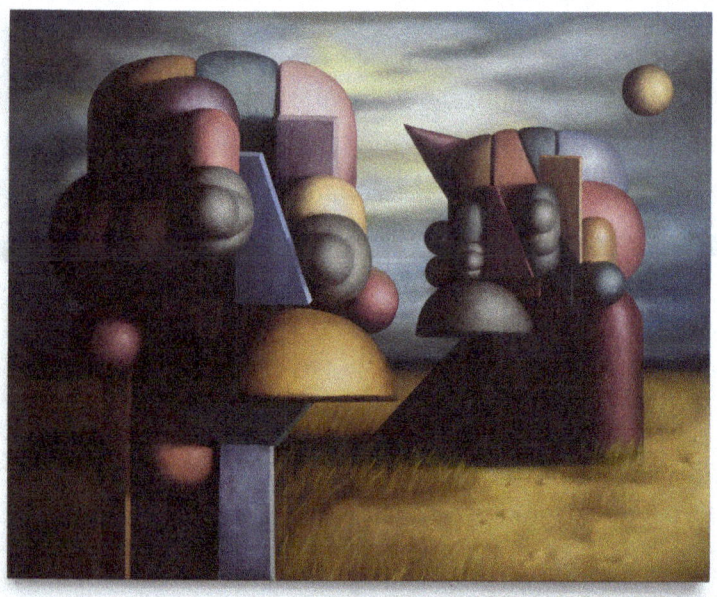

Aaron: I think there's a tendency for people, especially art writers, to assume that the final form of a painting is an accurate reflection of the way it came into being. So when one looks at a Jackson Pollock, for example, the work reflects the action of creation. But what's interesting to me when you describe your process is that even though you create forms that are quite substantial and solid, there's also a sense of indeterminacy and responsiveness behind their evolution. There's an undercurrent of instability, and an honesty in that.

Devon: I think when you try to maintain a certain level of control, it will always fail, over and over again. Not being from the most traditional artist background, I have this flexibility of understanding, going between saying "I know what I'm doing" and "I don't know what I'm doing."

Aaron: I think that ability to surprise yourself is important. And coming from a non-traditional background, it seems that there's a real freshness in how you're reaching back to Old Masters.

Devon: A lot of my recent portrait-type works were inspired by Dutch and Flemish masters. And so the figures themselves are connected to the historical figures they painted. Those images carry a lot of weight.

Aaron: In a way, you're creating new figures or icons for us to put our faith in, or to re-examine our faith. But, importantly, you're not creating idols.

Devon: Right, they are never meant to be all powerful. That humility undercuts and erodes any other impulse. You can speak about what you see and what you believe. I'm able to speak about what I see and what I believe. And the painting is this third-party object, it doesn't create this tension between us.

Aaron: So the works are speaking, but there's also space for silence.

21. Tom Gick: Beauty Abides

Tom Gick was born and raised on a farm in Indiana by devout Catholic parents, often escaping into the vast surrounding fields. He attended Purdue University and began writing and eventually painting. After years of traveling, he settled in Massachusetts and then Maine, where he has lived for the past thirty-five years. Over decades he has produced dozens of major paintings, often at large scale using household materials. After choosing not to sell or exhibit his works for many years, he is now preparing for multiple exhibitions.

Aaron: Your work comes from a deeply personal place. Years ago, you had a profound experience that shaped you both spiritually and artistically. Could you describe that?

Tom: I could not remember ever working figuratively in my early years. Then, to my shock, my grandmother poured through me (Figure 21.1), an experience somehow so frightening that I fled the studio for over a year. I sensed I was painting a presence that knew everything about me, and that I was being radically exposed, that she had come to put an end to love that hurts.

The following year I reentered the studio to die. After fifteen days—unable to eat or sleep, my mind desperately trying to give solace to my broken life—I finally collapsed and gave up my life in radical surrender. From the base of my spine, a river of orgiastic fire swept up my body and crashed into my skull. And ecstasy and love poured over me. This continued weekly for eight years, a literal dying of body and mind transforming all that is real. And all I could do was abide, as words and paintings poured out.

Aaron: Has your grandmother remained a presence in your work?

FIGURE 21.1

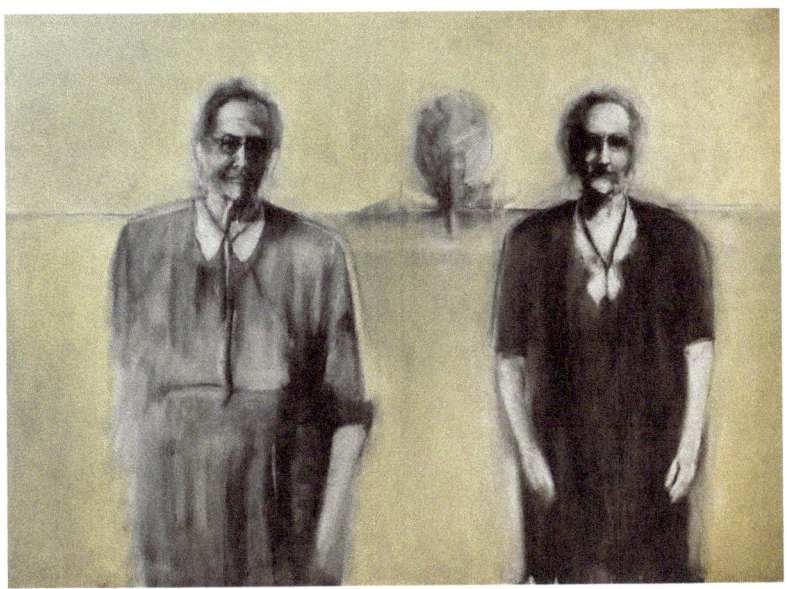

Tom: I rarely painted this grandmother figure again, but I began painting a younger female figure. I sometimes think of them as grieving mother and lost daughter. But I am often mistaken in trying to name what is unnameable.

Aaron: In your studio is a massive canvas that merges image and text (Figure 21.2). It crosses genres, from poetry to prayer. Can you describe that work and share some of what you wrote?

Tom: The script was originally written during my second night in the hospital as a doctor was trying to tranquilize me back to the world. Without thought, page after page poured out as fast as I could write. I think it says in raw and simple words all I will ever come to know or desire. Years later, I transcribed It onto this huge canvas, adding a later poem that is perhaps a response to its prayer. I have recently come to believe that this text is the voice of the grandmother singing solace beyond transformation:

> Through Union to Hope to Liberty,
> welcome home, Holy Spirit,
> to the open palm holding the field of our being.
> And it is all alright,
> for you could not have known
> it is impossible to hurry.

FIGURE 21.2

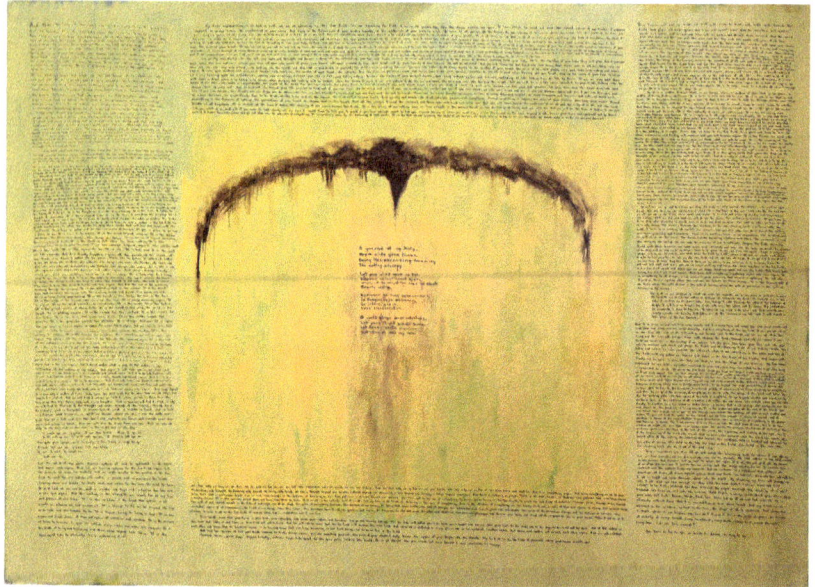

Aaron: What is your working process like? Do you think about or plan the imagery in advance, or does it tend to emerge gradually?

Tom: I rarely sketch or draw. Many of my canvases begin with words, later concealed with layers of translucent color. While I work, I know not what I am doing. Only as it emerges do I bring my mind and heart to the process, wishing only to help beauty to abide. It is my only answer to exploration, to the shock of what is unknowable and unnameable: unity with the divine.

Aaron: I know Rothko is a major influence for you. There are some parallels between you, both in how he seeks to encompass viewers in color and in his predilection for dark, smoky forms. When did you begin to notice Rothko's influence?

Tom: Years ago I first saw a large golden canvas of Rothko's. What most struck me was the sheer beauty of the surface. This surface beauty that invites embrace is what I most care about and hope to achieve. For it is intimacy one most relishes, to look into another's eyes and know.

Aaron: Have any other painters had a similarly powerful effect on your practice?

Tom: I have perhaps intentionally not exposed myself to much art. Early on, I remember being startled and captivated by the later water lily paintings of Monet. And certainly I would add Rembrandt and Vermeer.

Aaron: It's interesting that you look to a paragon of abstraction, Rothko, but also great figurative masters. It feels to me like your work hovers between abstraction and figuration. Is that how you would frame it?

Tom: I don't think I move between abstraction and figuration. "At the edge of flesh beauty waits," I once wrote in my poem "Flight of the Lark." The years of painting abstractly have determined the tools I use—house brushes, rollers, even my fingers pushing flesh into image whether abstract or figurative.

Aaron: To me, your works evoke a strong visionary tradition in Western theology, especially Christian mysticism. What kinds of spiritual sources have you been drawn to over the years?

Tom: I spent years reading all I could find about kundalini experiences. Much of the literature warns of the damage they can cause unless one is prepared by years of guidance and spiritual practice. I had neither. A spontaneous eruption can lead to madness.

I was deeply influenced early on by Jung's alchemical studies, among others. Recently I mostly avoid "spiritual" texts and instead turn to poetry, which after all was one of my first loves. I think of Rimbaud, Rilke, Crane, Poe, and T. S. Eliot.

Aaron: You tend to work in relative isolation. How has the physical space and environment in which you work shaped your creative practice?

Tom: For many reasons, I live and work in isolation. Maine has been a place of refuge, a surround like the embrace of a grandmother, her forests and mountains like hands gently shielding eyes from the blinding splendor of creation.

Aaron: You have seldom exhibited your works. What kind of home do you envision for them? Where would they find kindred spirits?

Tom: I have no idea. Hopefully a place that offers solace.

22. Ezra Bookman: The Rite Way

Ezra Bookman is the founder of Ritualist, the first creative studio specializing in the design of rituals; the former artistic director for Lab/Shul, an experimental, artist-driven, God-optional Jewish community in New York City; and the youngest member of the board of directors of the Secret City, an Obie Award-winning arts organization.

Aaron: Your practice has a lot of dimensions. To me, the roles of artist and curator come to mind first, but also director, designer, and even coach. Is there a title you prefer?

Ezra: Honestly, all of the above. I feel less attached to a job description than to the question that has always driven my work: How does transformation happen? Right now, that question is manifesting through an obsession with ritual, particularly an exploration of why some rituals are more meaningful than others.

Aaron: I know you don't love to pin something as complex and profound as ritual to a single definition. But can you tell us what ritual isn't?

Ezra: Ritual is distinguished far more by internal orientation than external form, so it's not really for me to decide whether what you're doing is or isn't a ritual. But I think problems arise when we conflate ritual, habit, routine, and tradition. Each of these is unique, and they serve different purposes. Flattening ritual to just a function of repetition deprives us of its power to deepen the experience of life. It also makes us susceptible to corporations that co-opt the language of ritual to sell us their products.

Aaron: What makes a ritual work?

Ezra: The most important thing is having a clear intention. I break intentionality into three P's: purposeful (*Why* am I doing this?), personal (Why am *I* doing this?), and particular (Why am I doing *this*?). After that, I examine the effectiveness of a ritual through seven lenses, or "lines" on which it travels: story, place, poetry, time, body, symbol, and meaning.

Aaron: What is your favorite ritual you have designed?

Ezra: I wrote and exhibited a ritual performance-art piece called *Us* for Lab/Shul's Yom Kippur services (Figure 22.1). In the Torah, divine forgiveness on Yom Kippur was signaled by a red ribbon miraculously turning white. I wanted to interrogate whether, in the absence of magic and miracles, tangible proof of change can be possible today. So I dropped three thousand feet of red ribbon from the balconies above the worship space and instructed the community to pass it around until all twelve hundred people in the congregation were connected by the ribbon. We tried to turn it white. It didn't work. So instead, we turned to one another for accountability in the slow, difficult, and opaque work of transformation. At the end, people could snip a piece of the ribbon and write their intention on it to use as a tangible reminder throughout the year of the commitment they made. Years later, people tell me they still have their ribbons.

FIGURE 22.1

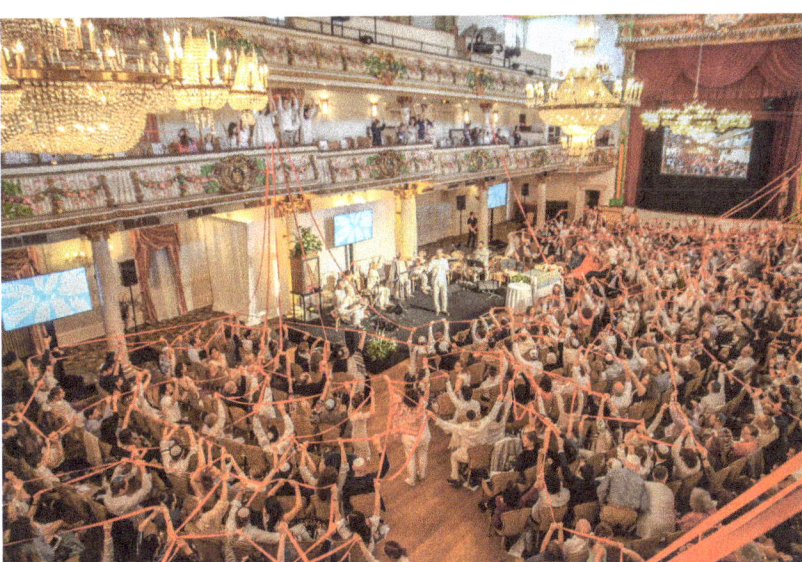

Aaron: People come to Yom Kippur with profound ritual expectations. Why is this such an important moment to think seriously about designing rituals for nontraditional times and spaces as well?

Ezra: Studies in behavioral science have shown that rituals increase feelings of control in times of uncertainty and create stable feelings of connection (Figure 22.2). We are living in a time of massive loss, uncertainty, disconnection, and change. Throughout human history, ritual has been one of our primary tools to navigate change, process grief, embody values, expand beyond ourselves, and envision a better future. We need ritual now more than ever, especially as we turn away from traditional institutions and toward new forms of belonging. I believe there is no such thing as a healthy individual without community or culture, and no such thing as a healthy community or culture without ritual.

FIGURE 22.2

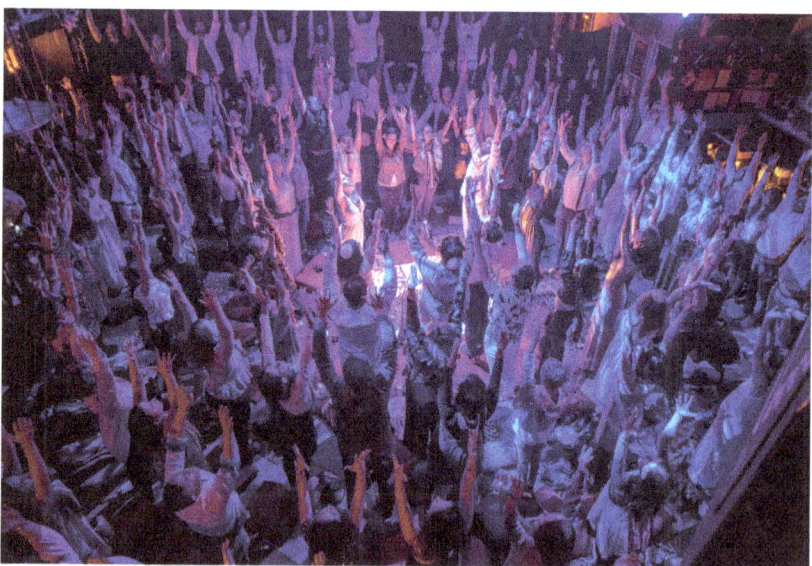

Aaron: When you consult with clients, especially corporate ones, how do you foster experiences that don't just become shortcuts for boosting productivity or job satisfaction?

Ezra: Rituals are friction. They're sort of the anti-shortcut. Taking a moment of gratitude before eating is functionally useless and makes lunch take longer, right? So before agreeing to an offer, I ask potential clients a lot about their values and goals. I'm looking for leadership, integrity, and a commitment to systemic policy changes, not just surface-level offerings, because rituals that express values that aren't practiced will breed a culture of cynicism and distrust.

Aaron: What would you say to those who feel their religious traditions provide them enough of a ritual buffet, so to speak, that they don't need to consider creating rituals?

Ezra: I'd say, "That's awesome. Tell me about some of the rituals you love the most." Eventually we might end up talking about how religious traditions have been creating new rituals and tweaking old ones throughout their history, and I'd encourage them to participate in that ongoing process in a way that feels authentic to them.

23. Sarah M. Rodriguez: Keeping Tracks

Sarah M. Rodriguez incorporates botany, anatomy, and anthropology in multiple-media work. She engages with interspecies communication, material experimentation, and ecology. Rodriguez received a BFA from California College of the Arts, an MFA from UCLA, and has attended the Skowhegan School of Painting and Sculpture in Maine.

Aaron: How has your cultural background contributed to your work?

Sarah: Half of my family is Native Hawaiian (Kānaka Maoli) and the other half were European settlers who moved to Texas. Both were formed by colonial ranching and agriculture. My family on Hawai'i lives in an area between one of the oldest ranches in the US and Mauna Kea, a colonial and ancestral site. Living in places with asymmetrical relations of power takes negotiation. So I've always tried to work by addition and not subtraction. Addition suggests assemblage, a formal strategy I try to make use of. While the balance of power might seem obvious in ranching (e.g., who works on the ranch, and who owns it) there is still some leveling out. Everyone literally has to get dirty at some point.

Aaron: Are there spiritual or ethical questions you struggle with over and over?

Sarah: I'm especially concerned with how we live and learn with animals. As an animal behavior consultant, I use procedures to change how an animal acts, so the ethical questions are direct but complicated. Just because we can train an animal to do something doesn't mean we should. We ask related questions in art, but it doesn't always feel as immediate.

The psychologist Susan Friedman addresses these issues in an exciting way, which reveals the established order as unnecessary. I think this is a collective task. She works with parrots and in the zoo world—another site I'd like to explore, as it has quite a bit of moral ambiguity and asymmetrical power structures. For me, working with canines involves rethinking punishment, coercion, and inherited social structures. Moving away from a punishment mindset, to me, is pretty radical. Humans are fluent punishers, and it changes our navigation in the world to let go of that.

Aaron: What drew you to working with animals? And can other species be artists?

Sarah: I see now how, even from a young age, I was always shaped by non-human animal relationships. Animals don't use signs or symbols; they mostly communicate through an index of information—scent, sound, movement. Attempting to think this way has changed me as a subject, and I'm constantly needing to hone my observation skills in order to be better at my profession in animal behavior.

FIGURE 23.1

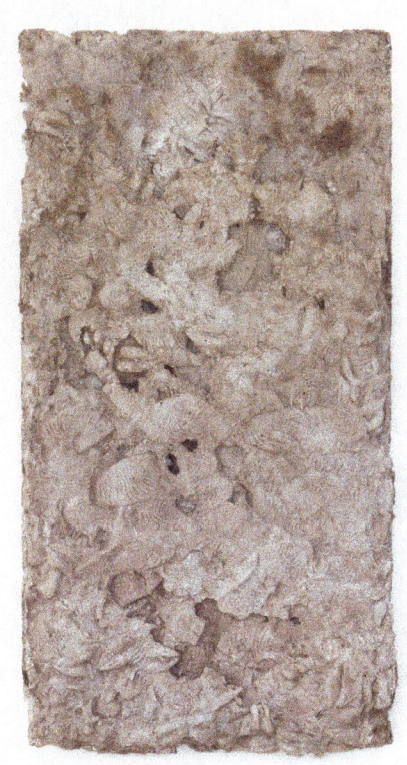

I hesitate to say that animals are artists, because I think that role is linked to a kind of labor that is specifically human. But they have things to teach us about art. Think about animal play, for example. Play requires role reversal and de-skilling, which seems like an important—though maybe undervalued—part of art-making.

Aaron: Your creative practice is informed by experiences like animal tracking, which is pretty unusual for an artist (Figures 23.1 and 23.2). What have these experiences taught you?

FIGURE 23.2

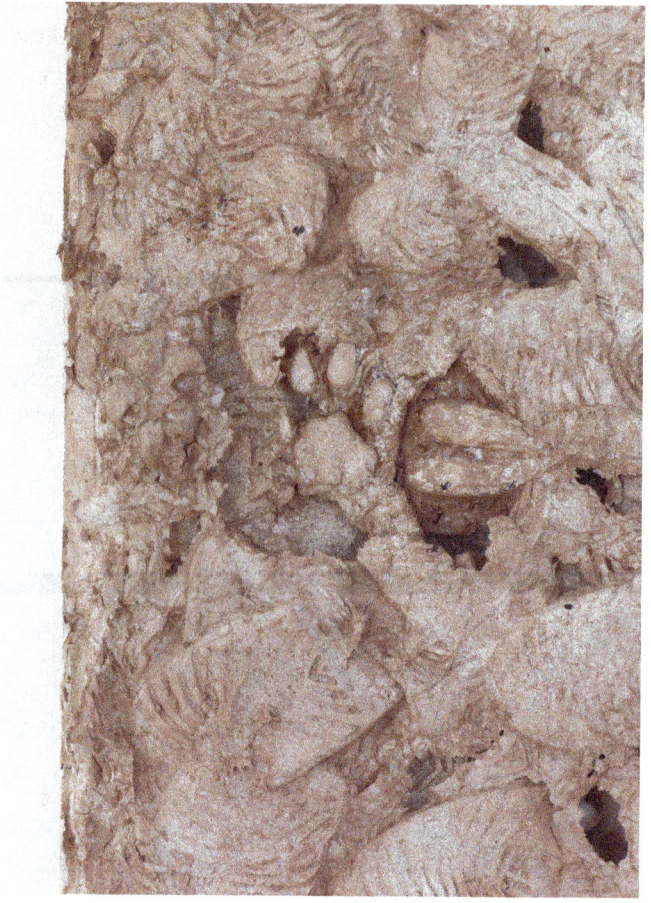

Sarah: Animals are a real thing and not merely a human abstraction. Animal tracking is empirical knowledge, so basically anyone in the world can participate. It's also predominantly male. In hunting, for example, the overarching narrative has something to do with power or a very linear idea of evolution. As I see it, we are constantly co-evolving with animals, which might have a spiritual implication.

Aaron: What do you think "environmental art" has got wrong and right? What new horizons do you see for how artists might engage ecology in the future?

Sara: I've seen some projects that impact native flora and fauna in detrimental ways. I'm also skeptical of art that requires you to make a journey to see a large piece in an otherwise untouched landscape. It's too similar to ideas of manifest destiny.

I'd like to see artists engage in collective futures for the environment (collective futures being a way of thinking that considers what a future looks like for the many, rather than the few in power). I don't think that necessarily needs to happen outdoors or in a natural setting. A site like a zoo can be such a slippery, interesting site for art-making.

Aaron: What has been the most surprising response to your work?

Sarah: When people expect it to have a specific message. I'm committed to the experience of art as nonverbal, as an exercise in knowing that the current order of things is not necessary or preordained. We are always becoming done and redone.

Homelands

24. MyLoan Dinh: Walking on Eggshells

*MyLoan Dinh studied visual arts at the University of North Caro-
lina at Chapel Hill and the School of Arts and Design at Wollongong
University New South Wales, Australia. She has exhibited internationally, and her work can be found in public and private collections in the United States and Europe, including the Muhammad Ali
Museum and Center, ArtFields, the Mint Museum of Art, and the
Imago Mundi Collection of the Benetton Foundation.*

Aaron: Can you talk a bit about where you were born and grew up?

MyLoan: I was born in Saigon. In 1975, during the last days of the US war
in Vietnam, my family and I escaped by sea. After moving between refugee
camps at Wake Island, Subic Bay in the South China Sea, and finally Camp
Pendleton in California, we were resettled by a Lutheran church in the Appalachian Mountains in Boone, North Carolina. One year later we moved
to Charlotte, where I spent most of my formative years. You could say I'm a
Southeast Asian American Southerner.

Aaron: How have you explored your experience as a refugee in your work?
Have you found yourself accessing different memories or understandings
of that experience over time?

MyLoan: My story as a refugee and immigrant is often a starting point in
my work. I've tried to learn to hold the specificity of my experience in tension with a desire to connect with universal dimensions of being human.

Both of these poles, of course, are subject to the slippery proclivities of the imagination, memory, storytelling, abstraction, and so on.

I was trained as a fine arts painter. From early on, my works referenced my culture and past—sometimes too much for my college professors. A professor once told me a self-portrait was too "ethnic," too "Oriental," and I was so young and impressionable I burned the painting. I wince now when I think about it. My name means phoenix in Vietnamese.

I recently completed a new work for the Benetton Foundation, *Return to Sender, Tent #8*, which integrates my eggshell work, a family photo from a refugee camp, and textile. The fabric is from the globally iconic cheap tricolor carryall—a symbol of migration with a checkered historical and political past. While recognized for their resilience, these bags are often given derogatory nicknames: "Ghana Must Go" bags in Nigeria; "Türkenkoffer" (Turkish suitcase) or "Vietnamesenkoffer" (Vietnamese suitcase) in Germany; "Guyanese Samsonite" in the Caribbean; "Bangladeshi bags" in England; "Zimbabwe bags" in South Africa; and "Chinatown totes" in the United States. With this work, I explore the material cultures of those evocative objects, with their partially hidden histories pertaining to class, ethnicity, race, and power.

Aaron: You've split your time between North Carolina and Germany in recent years. How does working in these different milieus inflect your work? Do you ever find the same piece taking on different shapes as it evolves across borders?

MyLoan: I feel very lucky to live and work in two vastly different places, Charlotte and Berlin. My husband is German. He's a choreographer and founder of Moving Poets, a multidisciplinary arts organization, so we spend time on creative projects in different countries. Geography certainly affects the creation of work. I grew up in the US South, which is predominantly and overtly Christian, in striking contrast to Berlin, which in my experience is very secular. Germans are very private about their religion, which is mainly Catholic or Protestant, and nearly half of Germans have no religion. I do take into account cultural and religious sensitivities when I'm exhibiting my work. Context is important. Sometimes I'll alter a work if I feel it will not read well.

Last summer I performed *Longing for harmonies* both in Charlotte and in Berlin. The thirty-minute performance installation includes a wedding dress, hazmat suit, paper parasol, ghost money, scissors, wooden beads, needles, eggshells, and an *áo dài* (a traditional Vietnamese dress): these are my symbolic protagonists. This performance makes public an array of private questions—of maternity, migration, culture, and history—and is haunted by centuries of prejudice against Asians and sexual violence against Asian American women. I wasn't quite sure how it would resonate in Berlin, because there is substantial English text and references to US colonial history. I did not change the work for the German audience. I was pleasantly surprised it resonated so well, even the nuanced bits.

Aaron: Has the recent spike in anti-Asian violence in the United States influenced how you talk about your work or the themes you explore?

MyLoan: Anti-Asian discrimination is part of the fabric of American colonial and imperial history (think of the Chinese Exclusion Act, Japanese internment camps, the Vietnam and Korean wars, and so on). Within our communities, we knew the tide was coming. And during the pandemic, after the ex-president used xenophobic rhetoric to scapegoat Asians, hate crimes against Asian Americans rose over 300 percent.

After the Atlanta spa shootings, as the nation confronted difficult conversations, my own response was intense. I have family and friends who work in nail service, so I was in intimate proximity to this horror. I created an installation titled *Treat Yourself.* I was reminded of the image of Christ washing the feet of his disciples. What was especially important to me, though, was how images of water, foot washing, and bathing span time and space (the US, Europe, Asia, the Middle East) and thus play into global entanglements. I thought about how, as a society, we haven't understood this lesson of humility and service: we don't know what it means to wash one another's feet, just like we haven't comprehended the meaning of "love thy neighbor." Only some are doing the washing.

Aaron: You often play with cultural inheritance, bringing both poignant and satirical elements into play, especially in your eggshell series. Can you talk a bit about the process and traditions behind those works?

MyLoan: Since 2016, I've increasingly used eggshell mosaics in my mixed-media work exploring gender and race. Covering objects in eggshells requires time-consuming labor, care, and focus—attention and intention. My eggshell-based work arose from formal experimentation and latent early exposure to *sơn mài* inlay lacquerware, an often overlooked traditional craft I saw growing up in a Vietnamese household (Figure 24.1).

FIGURE 24.1

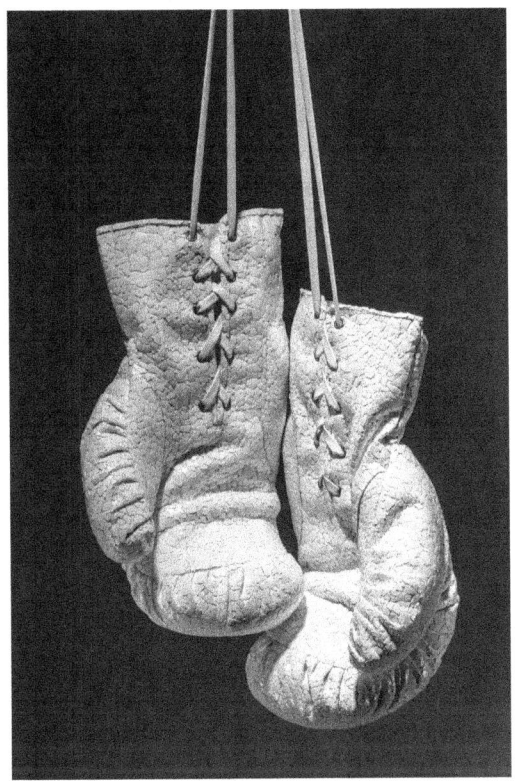

The interplay of materials and objects creates a dialogue between the collective and the individual. What is glimpsed between the cracks of the shells is as important as what is reassembled on the surface. The series probes a set of cultural tensions. Boxing gloves, though physically soft, bear connotations of violence and masculinity. Eggshells, by contrast, are traditionally associated with femininity and delicateness. Though fragile, they also evoke shelter, nourishment, and fertility. My first pair of eggshell boxing gloves was titled *Killing Me Softly*.

Aaron: Your work investigates both Buddhist and Christian iconography and themes. Are there key elements you find yourself revisiting in both traditions? Are there places where they intersect for you?

MyLoan: My relationship with religion is complicated and ambivalent, and my spiritual identity is conspicuously composite—I was raised in a traditional Southeast Asian Buddhist household and educated in public schools in the predominantly Christian US South. These geographic, social, cultural, and religious influences have significantly shaped my perspective. In my recent work I've been using prayer beads—rosaries and malas—in installations consisting of paintings of praying hands and physical objects. I want to find an opening for viewers to connect across cultural barriers.

Last year I created an installation titled *Zoom Buddha,* which channels the work of Nam June Paik. Communications technology has rapidly evolved since his legendary 1974 installation *TV Buddha*, yet questions to do with the role of the self in relationship to media and technology are increasingly relevant. The piece honors his legacy and reimagines his work in the context of the COVID pandemic, social media, AI, and virtual communication. Like Paik's, my Buddha gazes at his own image on the screen in an everlasting staring contest that raises questions of self and humanity.

Aaron: Another of your recent works also picks up Buddhist symbolism. Can you talk about your large *Thangka* piece?

FIGURE 24.2

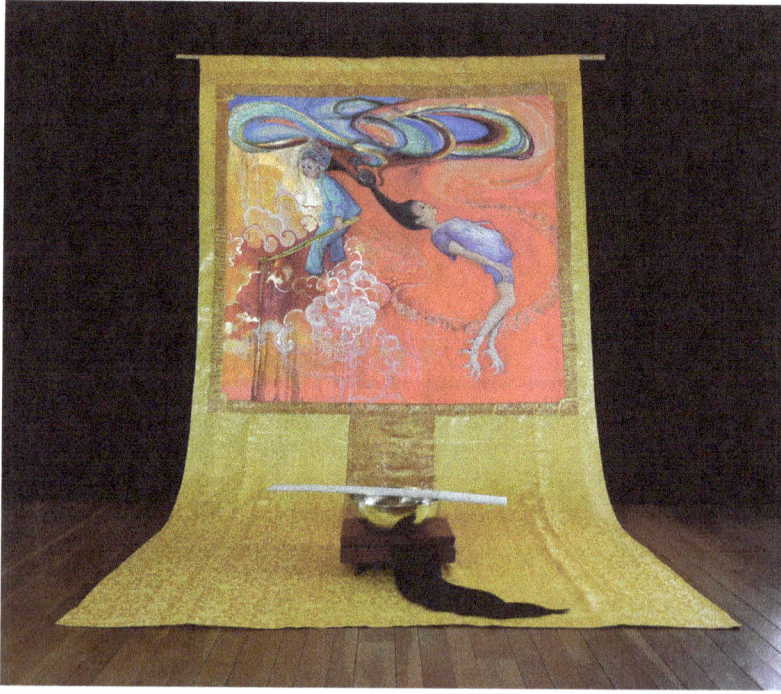

MyLoan: The installation is inspired by Tibetan thangka paintings, religious scrolls depicting a Buddhist deity or scene and used for personal meditation or instruction (Figure 24.2). Viewers are confronted by two figures, abstracted Buddhist iconography and cryptic hints of a mythology. One figure holds a sword that has been physically sliced from the scroll. The other figure hovers in transformation. Both are bound together by hair. Loose brush strokes and painterly drips surround them, suggesting another kind of visual language. In the foreground sits a stack of objects: a sword, metal bowl, and closed box with long black hair spilling from it. The sword is covered in eggshells.

Aaron: Turning more to process, do you have a particular ritual when working in your studio, whether straightforwardly religious or not?

MyLoan: Sometimes I burn incense and make a prayer before I start working. That's the most straightforwardly religious I get. I'm most spiritually centered when I'm intensely absorbed in work. Letting go of the "thinking" part of making allows me to subconsciously connect to something greater than myself. When I'm feeling deeply interwoven—entangled with the universe—I'm energized and yet at ease.

Aaron: Are there spiritual or philosophical questions you find yourself struggling with over and over in your work?

MyLoan: Questions of identity, consciousness, and othering are constant in my work, perhaps because they're at the root of many complex problems in society. I struggle with the contradictions between spiritual teachings and actual practice. Besides the unspeakable violence that's been levied in the name of religion, Christ and Buddha are too often invoked superficially. My work isn't intended to teach anything or claim any moral high ground. I don't even think I provide any conclusions. Rather, I hope to provoke the viewer to ask questions that I myself cannot answer. Sometimes there's a dark irony in my work. If there's any laughter, it's mixed with tears.

25. Emmanuel Osahor: Not Yet Eden

Emmanuel Osahor is a Nigerian-born Canadian visual artist based in Toronto. His practice engages with beauty as a necessity for survival and a precursor to thriving, depicting gardens as constructed sanctuaries that manifest attention and care. By prioritizing engagement with the beautiful, his paintings offer space for tending to the complexities of marginalization and inequality inherent in contemporary existence.

Aaron: Could you speak a bit about your experience immigrating to Canada and the perspective that has given you?

Emmanuel: In Nigeria, I watched a lot of North American TV, and given the way North America represents itself to the outside world, it's easy for a young person to believe that it is some sort of paradise, especially in contrast to the way the African continent is depicted in the same media. You start to think there is something wrong with your continent, because we are described as "developing," and North America is "developed." I thought this was because there were still extremes of poverty and marginalization in Nigeria, but once I arrived and started building a life in Canada, I realized that the same poverty and marginalization exist here. When you read the news more closely, you realize that, wait a minute, no one knows what they are doing!

Aaron: It sounds like this realization might have a spiritual dimension.

Emmanuel: It was profoundly influential, and I think it gets to the religious influence in my work, which is this experience of the "already and not yet." I've been struck by the immense beauty in the communities I have been a part of, both in Nigeria and now in Canada, as well as grieved by the levels of hardship people face because of injustice, and these days I often find myself not knowing what to do with this two-sided coin. The motif of the garden (Figure 25.1), which I explore in my work, has become a place for me to sit with this contradiction. Not to ignore it or provide solutions, but to just sit with it.

FIGURE 25.1

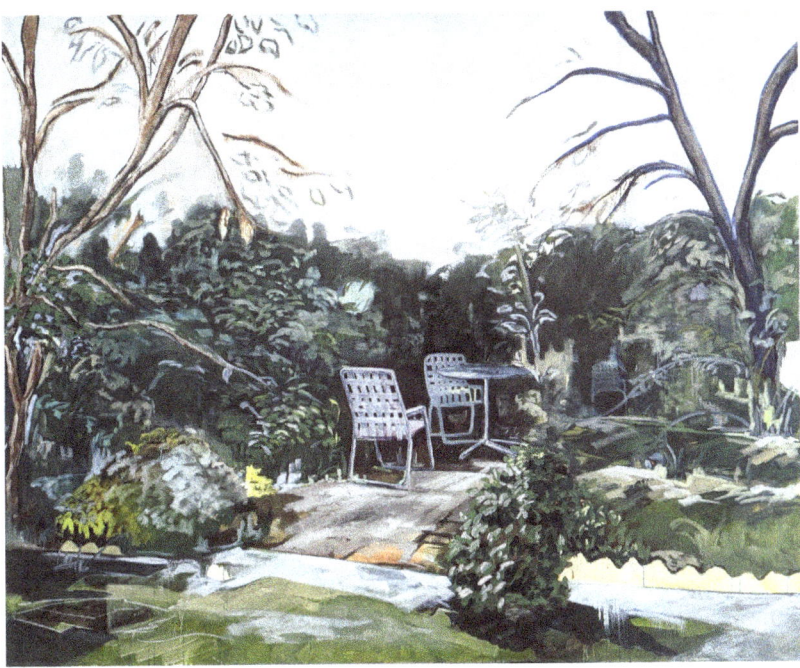

Aaron: Speaking of dislocation, and lost and regained places, do you think there's such a thing as "diasporist art," as the painter R. B. Kitaj suggested?

Emmanuel: I do, and it's a very important element of contemporary artistic practice these days. I think it is the American art historian John Peffer who talks about how contemporary experience is diasporic because most of us either have a personal experience of recent migration (ourselves, our parents, or our grandparents) or else "culture" has migrated to us (as in the impact of globalization on people living on their ancestral lands).

In the work of contemporary artists of African diasporic backgrounds, in particular, it seems clear to me that there is a navigation of multiple identities or worldviews. There is a restlessness and unease that actually becomes quite productive, because it manifests as a curiosity that invites you to not take your own or others' worldviews for granted. I think the diasporic artist has the capacity for a radical empathy. These artists make work that foregrounds their love for and desire for deeper connections to certain places and communities. I think it makes for work that is extremely compelling and reaches beyond ideological and other silos.

Aaron: What question do you find yourself struggling with most in your work?

Emmanuel: For me it's this notion of the "already and not yet"—and not just from a faith perspective. We live in societies where extremes of wealth coexist with extremes of poverty, where extremes of beauty coexist with extremes of hardship, where extremes of generosity and empathy coexist with extremes of anxiety, and community members fall through the cracks. Why? How? As an artist, I've always struggled with the reality that my role in society is to question, reflect, and invite people to question with me. I'm not a social worker or policy maker, and I'm very aware of the gaps in my own knowledge, so I don't hold a belief that I can fix anything. Instead, I try to make spaces for myself and others to sit with the tension. Maybe if we sit with it together, something might happen?

Aaron: You read a lot more theology than most artists I know. What theologians have your attention right now?

Emmanuel: I don't know that I read a lot of theology, but I've been lucky to have close friends and family who do, and most of my theological understanding has come from conversations with them. Funny enough, recently I listened to James K. A. Smith's *On the Road with Saint Augustine* as an audiobook in the studio while I worked. It was a revelation. I hadn't known that Augustine was a brother, a fellow African! And the notion that his theology and practice were influenced by his diasporic personhood was fantastic to discover. I'm also a fan of Richard Rohr's concept of "falling upward." It invites a radical perspective that I don't need to figure everything out but can trust that God is committed to me regardless of where I find myself. I find it challenging and never really know what to do with it most of the time, but I'm trying to make peace with that.

Aaron: Do you have a particular ritual when working in your studio, religious or not?

Emmanuel: Off the top of my head I would say no, but as I think about it, I'm always trying to be fully present when I'm in the studio, and depending on the season, I'll use different strategies to get there. If it's not too cold, I'll walk to the studio and use that time as a way to focus my mind on being present to the making. Sometimes I'll light a candle in the studio and sit still for a while. Other times, when I've got too much energy, I'll turn up the music and throw myself into the work—Afrobeat usually does the trick. The studio is a special place, and being able to spend my time making is such a gift. In a way, the making is its own ritual. When you are fully in it, you are not really thinking about the news or other anxieties anymore. Making can be frustrating, but the process is thrilling, and often you end up on the other side with something that surprises you, and you can't wait to get back to the studio.

Aaron: What has been the most surprising response that someone else has had to your work?

Emmanuel: I recently showed a painting titled *Lilacs (for Farah)* (Figure 25.2) of a lilac bush set ablaze by the sun and enveloping a wooden bench. I was referencing a photograph I had taken in the University of Guelph Arboretum. I remember the colors of the sun-blasted lilacs were so enchanting, and their perfume was intoxicating. I could not bring myself to sit on the actual bench, because I was afraid I would pass out from sensory overload. When I showed the painting, many people commented that all they wanted to do was sit on the bench. They wished they could enter the painting and stay there. That was profound for me, because rarely does the viewer feel the exact same way the artist felt when making an image. I don't want my work to be a one-to-one transcription of what I'm thinking. In fact, I am always hoping the paintings transform themselves and remain open for the viewer. But in this case it was a gift to see that the work was able to make an experience that I valued so palpable to other people.

FIGURE 25.2

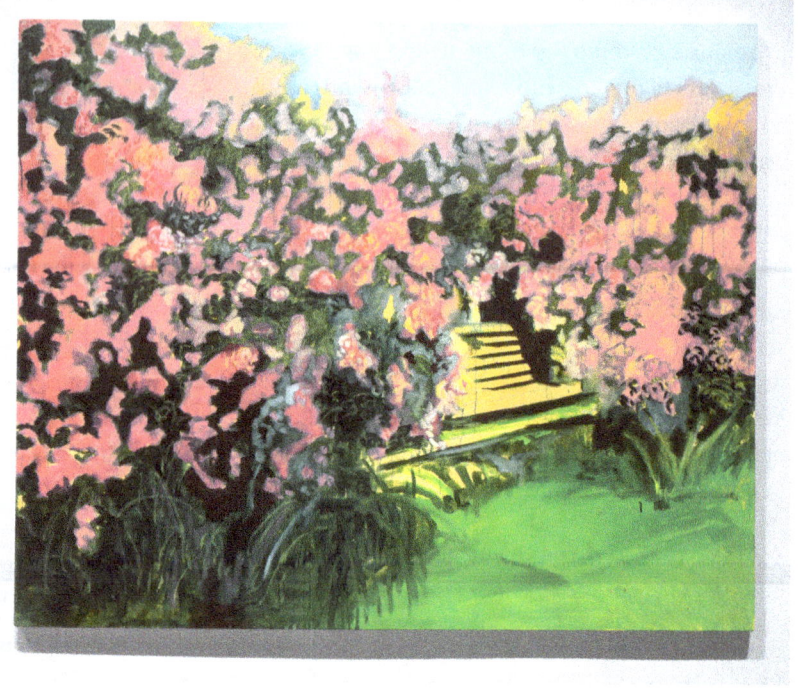

26. Eric Aho: Behind God's Back

Eric Aho is known for his paintings of the natural world. He studied at the Lahti Art Institute in Finland supported by a Fulbright Fellowship, the Central Saint Martins School of Art and Design in London, and the Massachusetts College of Art. His works have been exhibited widely around the world—including Cuba, South Africa, and Japan—and are in the permanent collections of institutions including the Metropolitan Museum of Art, the Museum of Fine Arts, Boston, and Buffalo AKG Art Museum.

Aaron: Could you speak a bit about how your cultural background has influenced your work?

Eric: The hyphen in "Finnish-American" is the defining detail—a disconnected, detached bridge between two cultures and centuries. My mother is Boston Irish Catholic, a special world in itself. We were raised, as my father liked to emphasize, in "Finland in America." Eventually, a Fulbright took me to actual Finland where I learned a great deal about myself and my family's history. The landscape is, among so many other things, about self-discovery, locating oneself in space, and exploring external forces. I'd painted the winter in New England prior to living in Finland, but there, snow and ice become an autobiographical subject. Like other Finns, I have a strong sense of communion with the woods and the natural world. There's also a hyphen of sorts between realism and abstraction.

Aaron: The natural landscape of New England plays a crucial role in your work (Figure 26.1). Have you found yourself looking at it in different ways over time?

FIGURE 26.1

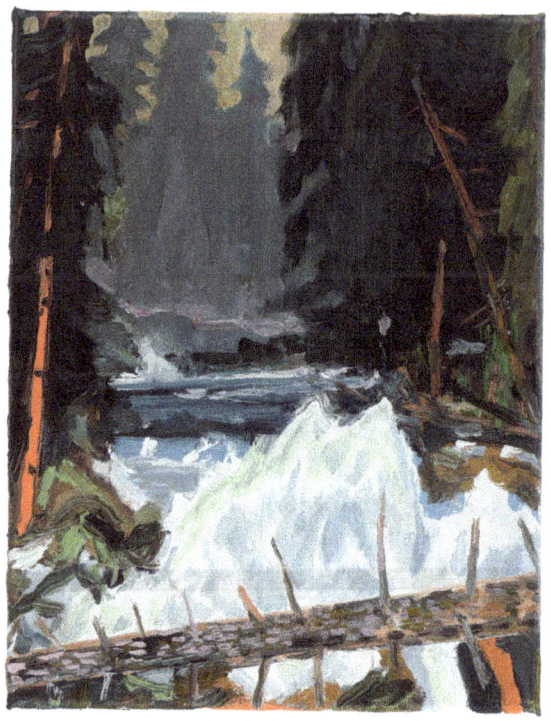

Eric: The northern New England landscape is central to my painting. But I don't think that's what the paintings are about. Initially, I painted the landscape more empirically, loosely for sure, but rooted in close observation. After twenty years of this fact-based approach, I discovered I was looking less at the landscape itself and more at the topography evolving on the canvas—it's like the painting became the place, like a plug was pulled from reality that existed independently.

In one of my first series from 1990, I painted along a stream deep in a hemlock ravine. I was new to Vermont and to painting. This past pandemic year I returned to a similar ravine with wild raging streams, but the interior I'm painting now is more my own and less the forest's.

Aaron: What is your process like in the studio? Do you have any rituals? How do you begin a painting?

Eric: I certainly have habits that have become rituals. I walk with my dog Elli to the studio following the same route. Once there, I sit and look at what happened the day before. Sometimes I listen to music (I like trying to sort out the differences between conductors handling the same piece) but mostly I prefer the quiet of the studio mixed with incidental noises of passing cars, dogs, and occasional chainsaws. At three, I stop for coffee and take another long look. Big decisions are often made looking with coffee in hand.

I try to start paintings differently each time. Sometimes I begin with a very quick drawing in charcoal on the primed canvas. This winter, on a large canvas, I made a more elaborate drawing to start, indicating more of a plan. The resulting painting was a surprise and felt like a totally new experience. That approach isn't habit just yet, and I don't think it's always wise to have a plan.

Aaron: What is the significance of absence, or the void, in your compositions?

Eric: I cut a hole in the ice each winter, an extraordinary black trapezoid—*avanto* in Finnish—intended for the bracing plunge to follow the extreme heat of the Finnish sauna. The shape carries so much personal meaning (Figure 26.2). It recalls my father's vivid stories of Depression-era ice harvests, and the chromatic black shape itself is a fundamental element of painting, a neural branch of a painter's family tree grafting me to Gustave Courbet, Kazimir Malevich, Agnes Martin, and Ellsworth Kelly. Above all, it's strange—a hole cut into the veneer of reality. And it's beautiful, but full of contradictions: simple and deep; protean and man-made; darkly black and filled with color; concrete and transitory; real and symbolic. I like that the shapes oscillate between the material of the paint, the image of a hole in the ice, and then just shapes in and of themselves. These paintings allow for unexpected ways of thinking about life's trajectory through the observation of form and color, culminating in a mysterious and inescapable vanishing point.

Aaron: You've mentioned the phrase "behind God's back." Where does that come from and how do you approach it in painting?

FIGURE 26.2

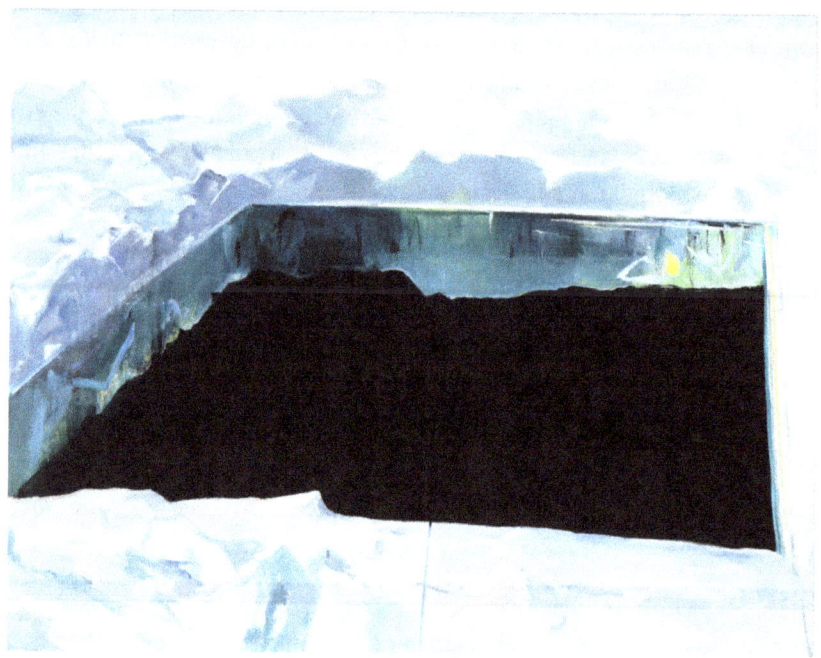

Eric: There's much poetry in the book of Isaiah where I think it has its origins. The phrase as I know it comes from the Finnish idiom "Jumalan selan takana," which first appeared on early hand-drawn maps of the region to indicate uncharted northern outposts. To me, it refers to a world outside civilization, a place unknown, almost secret. When I'm deep in the action of painting, there's a feeling of having stepped away from reality momentarily, into the unknown, like I'm working behind God's back.

27. Shahed Saleem: Adaptation and Innovation

Shahed Saleem is an architect, artist, and author, whose work explores migration and diasporas, in particular their relationship to loss, place, and reconstruction. His drawings and sketchbooks are held in the collection of the Victoria and Albert Museum, where he also created the first Ramadan Pavilion.

Aaron: You created a pavilion for the Venice Architecture Biennale in 2021 (Figure 27.1). Can you talk about this work and how it came about?

Shahed: The pavilion I co-curated for the Victoria and Albert Museum at the Biennale was titled *Three British Mosques,* and it told the story of three

FIGURE 27.1

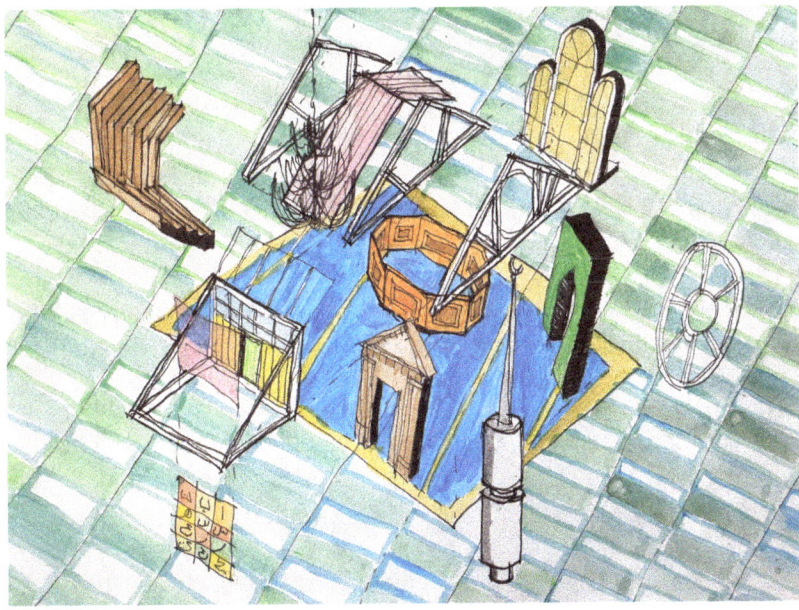

mosques in London that had all been created through the adaptation of existing buildings (Figure 27.2)—an eighteenth-century Protestant church, a nineteenth-century Victorian public house, and a 1930s suburban house. We re-created 1:1 replicas of architectural elements from each mosque, showing how the existing architecture had been adapted by the mosque community, in so doing creating a completely new visual culture.

FIGURE 27.2

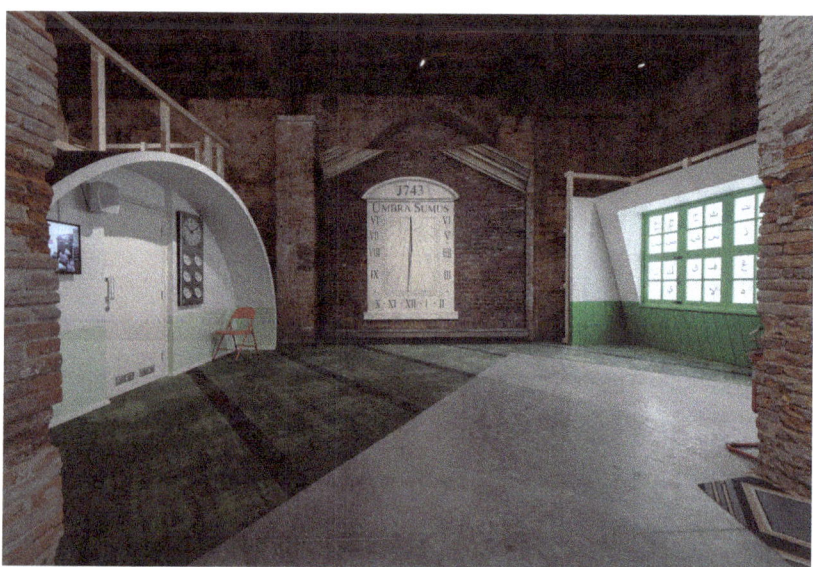

My book on the architectural and social history of the British mosque came to the attention of the V&A,[1] and we started talking about how that history could be represented by the museum. The Biennale pavilion was a great opportunity to develop this dialogue, and the museum has acquired elements from the mosques that we displayed.

Aaron: Was there anything that you worried over, or thought might risk misunderstanding, as you developed this project?

Shahed: We saw the work as a way of recognizing, documenting, and celebrating the contribution Muslims have made to British architecture. However, there is a fine line between a meaningful representation of Muslim experience and an exoticization of a less-understood "other." I feel that

---

1. Saleem, *British Mosque.*

since the project came from a place of lived experience and constituted part of a lifelong process of working out an expressive diasporic language, it was sufficiently in touch with people's experiences. Perhaps the tension between earnestness and fakery even gave the project its energy.

Aaron: You're an architect yourself and have designed mosques and Islamic community centers in the UK. Why did you choose to focus on the less-heralded forms of adapted mosque spaces? And why these three in particular?

Shahed: Some 80 percent of mosques in Britain are in adapted buildings. This means that the architecture of the British mosque is being determined by myriad existing spaces, built forms, and visual languages. To me this is a fascinating situation, where the mosque becomes an unexpected architecture, having been designed through a series of improvised and iterative design decisions, usually by the users themselves. I see this as a highly creative process resulting in a radical architecture that breaks established rules of design and taste. I find this exciting from the point of view of design and visual culture, but I also feel there is a certain power in that the diaspora is speaking through its own voice. We chose these three mosques as they each represent a certain type of adaptation: a residence, a former religious building, and a public house.

Aaron: Do you see parallels between the aesthetic and religious decisions of the Muslim communities you featured and those of diasporic communities of other faiths as they've adapted spaces?

Shahed: Minority faiths in Britain have always started their architectural journey by adapting existing buildings and creating their religious spaces in improvised and ad hoc ways. In this way, the architecture of the mosque is following the architectural history of Catholic, Nonconformist, and Jewish communities in Britain over the previous couple of centuries.

Aaron: Returning to your own practice, what lessons do you draw, whether stylistically or otherwise, from these kinds of domestic religious spaces?

Shahed: I'm driven by the question: How do we design new mosques in Britain that are a continuation of the design history laid out by the adapted religious buildings of the past century, rather than a rejection of this history in favor of a set of global Islamic architectural referents? This latter option is becoming more and more popular for new mosques, but I'm most interested in exploring the first option.

Aaron: What do you think is most challenging and exciting in mosque design today?

Shahed: The question of what defines an "Indigenous" mosque has recurred throughout the history of mosque design in Britain, and indeed the West more broadly. I think seeking an architectural voice that responds to and represents the complexity of the diasporic condition is still an outstanding and exciting challenge.

Science and Medicine

28. Stephanie Rayner:
The Heartbeat of the Cosmos

Stephanie Rayner is a multimedia artist whose work engages with the transformation of spirituality by science and technology. Born in Toronto, she spent ten years traveling the globe overland before beginning her art career. She has lectured at the Vatican Symposium on Religion and Science (Malta), the First International Symposium of Religion and Science (University of Toronto), Stanford University's Center for Advanced Study, and multiple art institutes in China.

Aaron: Could you describe the moment when you knew you would become an artist? Would it be fair to call it epiphanic?

Stephanie: I take the word *artist* very seriously. I am not an artist until that flame within me is lit. So, the beginning of, and the commitment to, each major artwork contains that moment. I need to continually become an artist, to reimagine myself. I let imagination nourish the mysterious becomings within the soul.

But, yes, there was one particular moment. I was young enough to be carried in the crook of my father's arm. At dusk, all of a sudden, a tree on the far side of the garden glows gold. Through my eyes I am pierced by beauty. I crumple forward.

Aaron: You've spoken about how your travels around the world became a springboard for your art. Could you talk a bit about some of the more spiritually compelling experiences on these adventures?

Stephanie: My travels began before cell phones and computers. If you had the will, there was a way to go back in time. If you could ride a horse, if you could tough it out, you could visit remote places with ancient energies, energies not of the twentieth century. For fifteen years, I traveled paths less taken: temples entangled by jungles, mountain shrines, deserts. In these places, sometimes, the veils do lift.

On a trip overland across North Africa, I rode across part of the Sahara starting at Giza. Sitting on my horse, quiet and alone between the giant paws of the Sphinx, my vision was fixed on the horizon point where those unblinking eyes had been focused so fiercely for millennia. Then I heard a *chunk, chunk, chunk.* I moved the horse from between the huge paws to see (hooves in sand make no sound). A young man and woman were digging a grave beside the Sphinx for a tiny, tightly shrouded baby. The juxtaposition between that powerful, timeless, indifferent stare and the poignant measure of that moment is bound to the core of my being.

Aaron: You use highly unusual materials in your work, from raven's wings to an artillery shell, vertebrae, maps, and even DNA sequencing gels. Do you find yourself saving objects and then finding uses for them, or rather thinking of what a specific work needs and then searching for the right objects?

Stephanie: Some materials find me; others I search for. The materials for *Angel Dancing on the Head of a Pin* took me to an illegal arms fair. Later, I had to carry a rectangular clear plastic package of white powder—dental amalgam—through a drug gang area of Toronto, with no purse or pocket to hide it in. It took five years to find a truck-smacked raven (it's illegal to deliberately kill ravens in Canada, so I needed one that was already dead), and then I had to finger-lick all the barbules back together on both wings. Other materials just fell into my hands.

Aaron: Are there objects that have felt too sacred to use in your work? Or objects that suddenly seemed to become sacred when you placed them within a work?

Stephanie: Ah, what adventures we will miss in not telling of the procuring of profane materials!

FIGURE 28.1

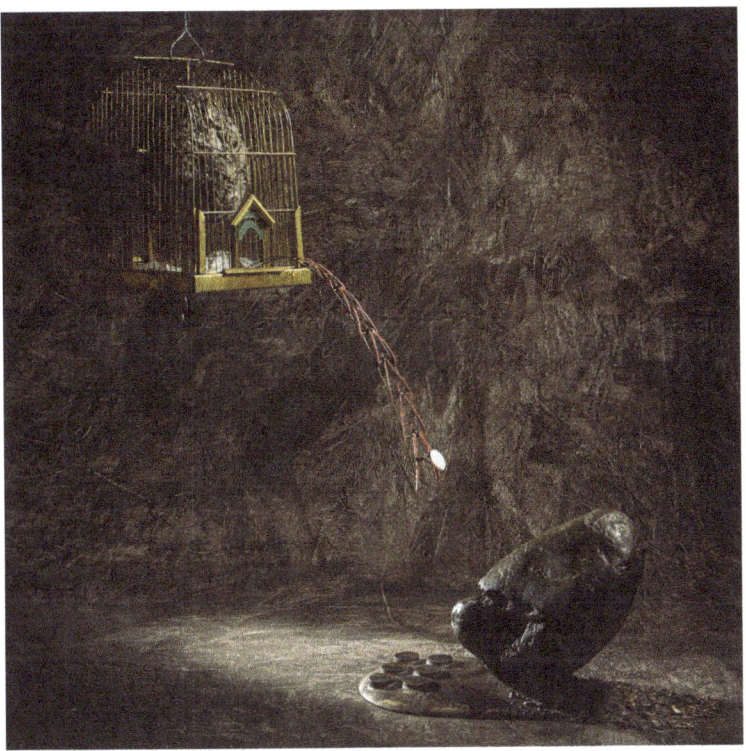

Of the sacred there have only been two. In my work *Dialogue of the Two Chief World Systems* (Figure 28.1)—which takes its title from Galileo's radical tome—there is a rusting fourteen-carat-gold-leafed birdcage. It has church doors at each end. Within the birdcage is a gold cross on which there is a wasp's nest the size of a human head. The paper of the wasp's nest is made of chewed-up pages from the New Testament. I could not tear up the Bible I owned. It is the kind of Bible with gossamer pages, all gilt edged. To do the tearing I had to (and the irony here is not lost on me) steal a Gideon Bible from a hotel room bedside drawer.

The other sacred object is a graph printout of a dying human heart. You can see the path of that heart's struggle up the mountains of that graph only to flutter, fail, fall, and then struggle up again. There are handwritten notes at intervals done by the attendant—for example, "the patient blinked."

I am not sure yet if or how I will use the map of this journey in a work of art. It was to be paired with NASA's pulsar radio signals that sound like a heartbeat from the universe. I hold it in keeping with great reverence and tenderness. My eyes tear up each time I look at the end.

Aaron: In many of your works, research plays a strong role, and you're often in touch with leading scientists in experimental fields from genetic research to astrophysics. What have you learned from these encounters, not just scientifically but perhaps spiritually or artistically?

Stephanie: I have been deeply inspired by scientific discussions and projects I was allowed access to, and in return I found scientists who were enthralled and moved by seeing their work transformed into visual poetry by the power of metaphor. I think of the great generosity of spirit and respect from people like Dr. Chris Corbally, a Jesuit and former director of the Vatican Observatory Research Group, and Dr. Alan Davidson of the University of Toronto, who worked on the Human Genome Project and was recently part of the team developing the gene-editing technology called CRISPR.

I've learned that art, science, and religion are still fueled by ancient desires for a dialogue inherent in the mystery and magic of creation and destruction. And, as many myths reveal, we have an abiding desire to steal a portion of that power.

Once you explore the revelations of science—the multiverse, black holes, dark matter, quantum physics, the photographs of far galaxies sent back by the James Webb telescope—there is a realization that in our era humankind is experiencing the birth of a profound new consciousness. All births are painful and contain elements of danger and risk, but births are the necessary threshold for evolving potential.

In some cases, my work deals with the perceived pitfalls of the Trickster's gift of technology, while other works, I believe, disclose the possibility of a bridge between science and spirituality, a bridge not based on any one culture's interpretation of God, but rather the sacred as revealed through universal phenomena that bind us to the cosmos.

And as to our ancient desire for that dialogue, we now use hugely powerful artificial eyes and ears to slowly scan the heavens, waiting for a sign.

Aaron: I had the privilege of talking with you in front of your *Boat of Eternal Return* (Figure 28.2). How have people responded to that work, especially spiritually?

FIGURE 28.2

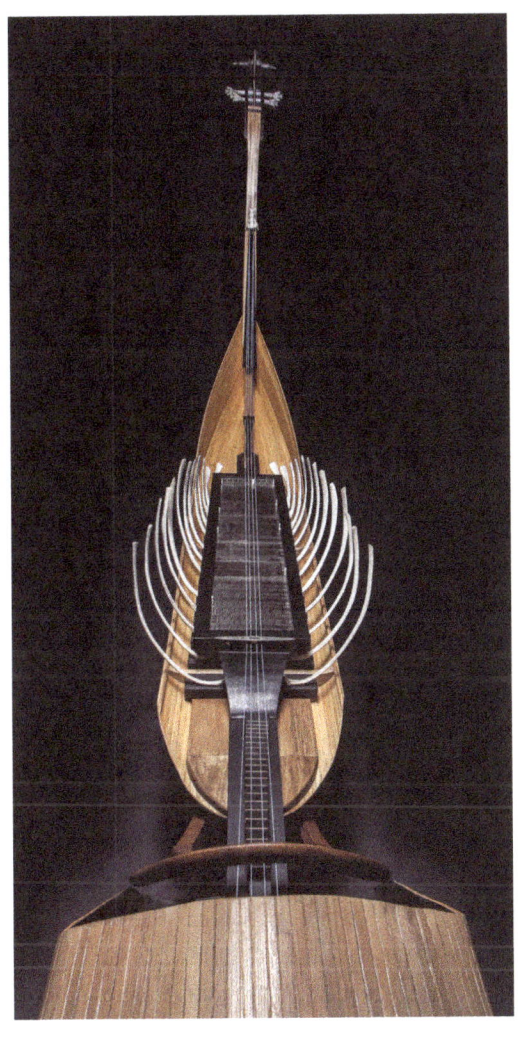

Stephanie: There is a silk scarf that travels with the boat. Four Buddhist nuns traveled from the residence of the Dalai Lama in Dharamshala, India, to see the *Boat of Eternal Return* in a Toronto art museum. They walked around it four times chanting, then knelt beside it and prayed for the boat to bless them. Then they sang prayers standing in front of the high prow, and at the end of that hymn, Maio Lin draped the keel with the silk scarf to bless the boat on its long journey.

There is a book that travels with the boat, in which people write comments about their experiences with it. After reading it, as one curator said, "People don't just write their names; they pour out their souls in essays!" One viewer wrote, "You have looked into the eyes of my soul and played the strings of my heart." Another wrote, "I know one day I will float in the embrace of those ribs of the boat. But now when that boat comes, I will not be afraid. How graceful and deep this Peace Inconceivable." Another called the boat "a gondola on which spiritual seekers, shamans, and mystics can move to the spirit world without the normal requirement of death."

29. Hanae Utamura: Life Breaths

Hanae Utamura is a Japanese interdisciplinary artist working in video, performance, new media installation, and sculpture. Her work seeks to connect human beings and earth, using the body as a conduit. She reflects on our relationship to nature, focusing on how we imagine, experience, and affect the natural world through scientific development and historical narration. She received her Master of Fine Art at Chelsea College of Art and Design, and her Bachelor of Fine Arts at Goldsmiths, University of London. She was based in Buffalo, New York at the time of this interview.

Aaron: Can you talk about how you came to connect science and spirituality in your practice?

Hanae: I think it is related to the environment where I grew up, in the industrial city of Hitachi, in Ibaraki prefecture in Japan. Hitachi company started there, and it used to be a major city for copper mining. The Hitachi mine chimney, the tallest chimney in the world, was erected there in 1915 to avoid the damage being caused by pollution released at lower heights. It was one of the first examples in Japan of civil protest winning out against a company and resulting in a change.

On the other hand, Hitachi is between the Pacific Ocean and mountains, so there was a lot of nature around me. Also there is Oiwa Shrine, located under the sacred mountain called Oiwa. It's become quite well known as a place of spiritual power in recent years. It has a rare style of *Shinbutsu-shūgō* (a syncretism of Shinto and Buddhism) and is dedicated to 188 gods.

Aaron: Shinto has a long and complex history in Japan, including a period in the twentieth century when it was closely tied to the state, and the emperor in particular. What does it mean to you to engage with Shinto practices and beliefs now, and what aspects do you find most compelling?

Hanae: Before modernity was introduced by foreign countries in the mid-nineteenth century, Japan was closed to the outside for about two hundred years. Shinto allows me to be in touch with the sensibility and connection to the environment of that earlier time. A Shinto shrine honors the place where it is situated as a god. A lot of my projects are site specific, often honoring the history and spirit of the place, and that is greatly influenced by Shinto.

A shrine also protects a place from human intervention—and shrines are often built in places that play important roles in the ecosystem, such as providing water or fostering a symbiotic relation between forest species. In the process of modernization, the Japanese government allowed the destruction of many shrines, and Kumagusu Minakata was the first environmental activist against this movement. He was a scientist, folklorist, philosopher, and environmentalist who did extensive research in fungi, dictyostelium, and slime mold in Nachi Forest in Japan. He also made the *Kumagusu Mandala*, a drawing that represents his conception of Western sciences and Mahayana Buddhism. He is an influential figure for me, bridging Western and Eastern philosophy.

Aaron: In *Teaching a Stone to Talk*, Annie Dillard reflects on the silence of a desacralized world. She writes: "What have we been doing all these centuries but trying to call God back to the mountain, or, failing that, raise a peep out of anything that is not us? What is the difference between a cathedral and a physics lab?" Would it be fair to say you're trying to teach stones to talk, or at least breathe?

Hanae: Yes, definitely. I feel that spirit manifests itself in material form. I am creating a framework where these voices can be expressed in concrete ways. My making process invites a lot of chance and contingency, and this is because consciousness affects material conditions, the form of the phenomenological encounter. In quantum physics, we know that the presence of the observer actually changes the result of the experiment. I think now is an interesting time, when the dialogue between religion and science—especially introspective practices such as meditation and material-based practices in scientific research—can advance our understanding of the world like a mirror.

Aaron: In your recent sculptures, you embed sediment from samples in the deep-sea floor, which seem to respire when you place them within hot glass (Figure 29.1). How does that work?

FIGURE 29.1

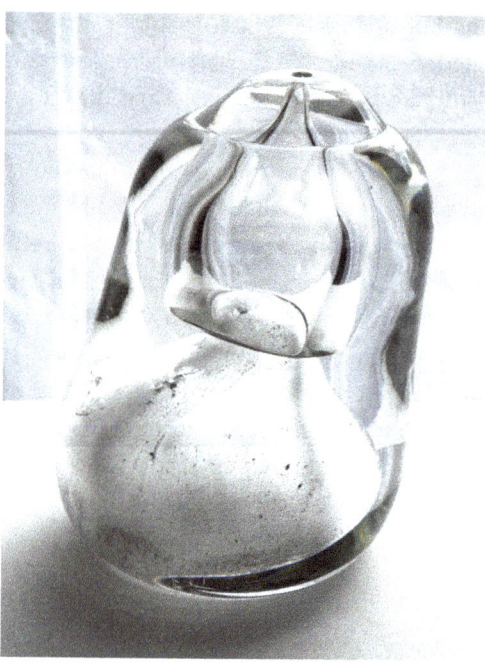

Hanae: When these sediments are put inside hot glass and sealed completely, some gas or air comes out because of the high heat. How it reacts varies depending on the sediments, and that's the fascinating part. I feel like different parts of the ocean are expressing themselves in various rhythms. Sediments are inorganic material, so most of them don't contain much carbon and therefore don't burn much, but some sediments contain more organic material, and they will blow air out of the glass from inside, sometimes even breaking it. In one instance, the glass expanded at the peak of its heat and then shrank when the temperature got lower—like a creature who breathes in and out.

Aaron: From your glass works to recent paintings, you're very interested in forms that encapsulate or shelter others (Figure 29.2). Has this been shaped by your experiences of motherhood?

FIGURE 29.2

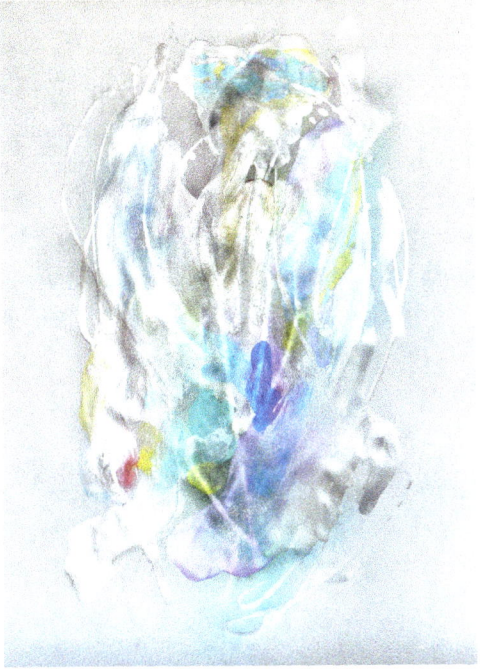

Hanae: I was thinking a lot about incubated bodies when I was pregnant. Unlike the external world, this internal world is not a visible one, but can only be felt. I try to capture that internal reality by tuning into my consciousness through breathing. I was also thinking a lot about the circulation of water and its memory, and in my work I let the water lead the way as a catalyst. Sixty percent of the human body is made of water, 80 percent with a newborn. The amniotic fluid in which the fetus grows is similar to seawater, which reminds us of life's origin in the ocean.

I made these watercolor works by looking at the glass works. I took inspiration from how the breath on top merges with the breath of the sediments from underneath the earth. I was also looking at how my breath, which at that point contained another life, was merging into the breath of the earth. These watercolors were inspired by these three components— earth, a life inside me and my body, and connecting these through the act of breathing in and out.

Aaron: I know you're also interested in exploring contamination and toxicity. What do you think we can learn from growth in inhospitable environments and conditions?

Hanae: I take inspiration from how plants tolerate nuclear radiation. One scientist speculates that this is because of an inbuilt memory from ancient times when radiation levels were higher than today. There is a microbe that eats plastic and another that eats nuclear waste. I am amazed at how nature can adapt and even thrive in those circumstances. I think we also find ourselves in the process of learning how to negotiate that toxicity. Toxicity points out and directs us to the real work needed in our society.

30. Adam Belt: Engaging the Infinite

Adam Belt's work has been exhibited nationally and internationally at venues including the Museum of Contemporary Art San Diego; Quint Gallery in La Jolla, California; Crystal Bridges Museum of American Art; Franklin Parrasch Gallery in New York; and RCM Galerie and Topographie de L'Art in Paris. His artistic practice is a contemplation of physical and phenomenological aspects of our world, the cosmos, God, and religion. An active member of the Episcopal Church, he lives in Carlsbad, California.

Aaron: You've spoken about your art practice as a form of calling or vocation. Are those terms you've always used to describe your work, or has that awareness emerged over time?

Adam: I recall that terminology developing early on, after I transitioned from traditional landscape painting to creating installation works using physical phenomena, like ice moving over a bed of sugar or paint flowing over panels. In my mid-twenties, I decided to attend graduate school in art. Before this, I'd had a sort of underlying understanding that art was a way to engage the mystery of the unseen—the infinite as expressed in the physical world—in a way that church and religion could not. The decision to pursue art helped codify this understanding for me.

Aaron: A lot of your work tackles both scientific and spiritual subjects. Do you find that one of those elements often comes first, or do they tend to coincide?

Adam: For me it's more that there is a space *beyond*, a space where there is no differentiation. That's where the work begins.

Aaron: You seem especially interested in elements that do unexpected things within spaces, like galleries, which are usually very controlled. Can you talk a bit about those processes and what kind of spiritual connections emerge through them?

Adam: I'm really drawn to natural phenomena, like crystals growing, or sand dunes drifting through the space, or a layer of fog suspended in the air. I love instances where the form is not derived from metaphor or necessarily deliberately shaped. The form grows through inherent, unseen forces and processes, influenced by conditions in the space like humidity, temperature, or even the movement of visitors. The sterile, often antiseptic environment of the art gallery or exhibition venue is ripe for contrast. The challenge is to foster an encounter that can defy visitors' expectations and create a work or experience that can really breathe.

Aaron: A number of your works reimagine traditional ritual objects such as baptismal fonts, reliquaries, or rosaries. Do you see these objects as having a liturgical function?

Adam: Often I am creating an object that I want to see in the world, and I don't think about context until later. I have created a baptismal font (Figure 30.1) for a church based upon a natural hot spring at Yellowstone National Park, but the crystal-growing fonts I've created elsewhere wouldn't work for use in church.

FIGURE 30.1

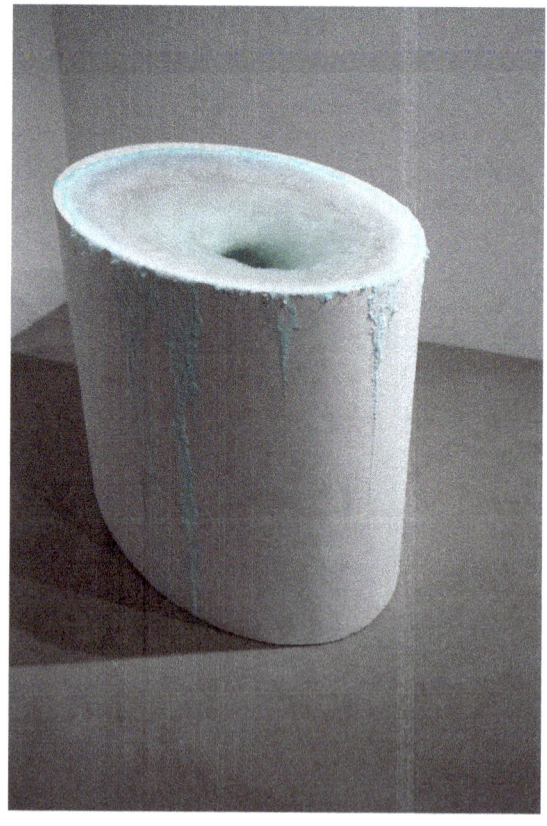

They're made with a man-made salt solution that forms crystals as the water evaporates, and while the fluid isn't dangerous, it's nothing you'd want to stick your hand into or ingest. (At shows, I always know who has touched the fluid by who asks me whether it's toxic.)

I've created a rosary of meteorites that is quite large, sort of Flavor Flav sized, but I would love to create smaller versions. Holding something from outer space in your hand and praying with it heightens the awareness of God's creation beyond your immediate surroundings. One idea that only exists in drawing form is *Altar of Ages*. The altar would consist of thirty layers of rock arranged in order of age, from 4.6 billion years old (from the Campo del Cielo meteorites) on the bottom to zero years old (from an I-5 freeway expansion) on the top. I did make a smaller work called *Rock of Ages* (Figure 30.2) composed of those same thirty layers.

FIGURE 30.2

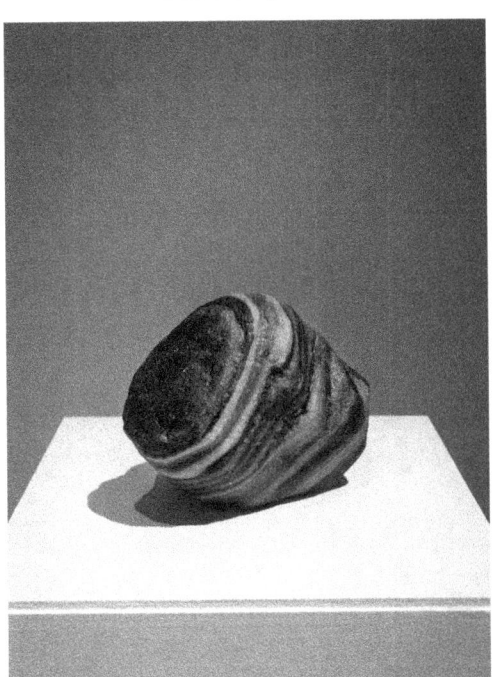

Aaron: What kinds of spaces would you like to see your work exhibited in?

Adam: I would love the opportunity to exhibit in and interact with sacred spaces. I think my work might be more fully realized there. The typical gallery context carries so many assumptions and burdens that come from the cultural conditioning and history of contemporary art. While there is a growing openness to the spiritual and religious, there is still a lingering and palpable taboo against it. Religious contexts open people up to the possibility and even expectation of a spiritual encounter, while also engaging an audience beyond the narrow contemporary art community. Outside of pre-ordained art spaces there exists greater possibility for surprise and wonder.

Aaron: What projects are you working on at the moment?

Adam: Currently I'm working on cast polyurethane resin blocks that interact with the light of the space they occupy. In one series, the blocks transition from an opaque white to transparent. I cast forty-five to sixty layers, calculating a varying amount of opaque white to create the ombre. My desire is to remove meaning and allow for presence to be the focus. This quote from Thomas Merton resonates with me in relation to this new direction: "But there is greater comfort in the substance of silence than in the answer to a question." Earlier I mentioned my intuition about art as a means to engage the infinite. That idea is at the core of this work.

31. Jocelyn Mathewes: Seasons of Inquiry

Jocelyn Mathewes is an interdisciplinary mixed-media artist whose work has been exhibited in galleries, museums, and community spaces across the US. She has participated in residencies with the Artist Residency in Motherhood, Makers Circle, and Stay Home Gallery. In 2020, she founded EAT/ART space, an alternative pop-up gallery. She organizes artist meetups in the southeastern US highlands to foster regional growth, collaboration, and innovation.

Aaron: I'd like to talk about how your artistic and faith journeys intertwine. Can you speak first about your religious background?

Jocelyn: Growing up in New England, we attended a Baptist church for a time, then an evangelical Protestant church. We were devout; our faith was central to how we structured our lives. Worship was a mixture of traditional hymns and contemporary music, and preaching was heavily emphasized.

My parents were eager to educate me on the history of the faith. We studied Reformation history and theologies of other denominations, as well as some comparative religion. We discussed the Protestant rejection of images in worship, among many other controversies.

I was homeschooled by my mother, who was an artist in her own right. She studied painting at Boston University and taught lessons out of our home, so I had an example of artistic exploration and religious practice to follow and admire.

Aaron: What do the rhythms of your life look like now, married to an Orthodox priest?

Jocelyn: I made the transition away from iconoclastic traditions when I encountered Orthodoxy in college and began to study art. Because artists think about the meaning of materials, I was naturally drawn to worship that made the material experience of worship into a feast.

When you are married to the priest, you are enmeshed in the life of the church. An Orthodox priest's vocation is all-encompassing and involves the whole family. We shape our lives—meals, school, vacations—around the liturgical rhythm of the church. It's intense and demanding, but the time we carve out for spiritual practice and contemplation is an anchor. My art practice flows out of the rhythm of faith, so I plan my time and husband my energy in response to and in support of these rhythms.

Aaron: Would you go as far as to say there's a liturgical character to your practice as an artist?

Jocelyn: The heartbeat and steps of my artistic process are just as liturgical as my prayer life. Repetition figures both in medium and in execution. I work in printmaking and photography, which are mechanical and slow, repetitive. Each one has its own particular series of steps at which you can add variation.

My art practice also ebbs and flows like the liturgical seasons. Here in Appalachia, we have four seasons. During the summer I spend my time making cyanotype prints; it's fastest and easiest when the sun and its UV rays are most intense. During the winter it's harder for me to be outside because of some medical symptoms that flare in the cold. So I stay indoors and work the prints into shapes or focus on different media. Ecclesiastes 3 comes to mind. "A time to print and a time to sew."

Aaron: Are there spiritually significant themes or imagery that recur in the work itself?

Jocelyn: Medical themes play a huge role—diagrams, organs, body parts, measuring tools, et cetera (Figures 31.1 and 31.2). Medicine has its own language and insights that feel very disconnected from the spiritual world, yet modern medical systems have played a large role in my healing from a chronic illness. I explore the gap between living in a body and the scientific analysis of bodies. In that gap I see faith create a deeper, integrative meaning, one that allows true and full healing.

Mapmaking is the second big theme—topography, cartography, and 3D elements. The three-dimensional structures I create are made from cyanotype prints that come from weeding my garden. The weed prints document the invisible labor of maintenance that goes along with healing from illness. All these methods try to describe and document that gap between medicine and faith.

FIGURE 31.1

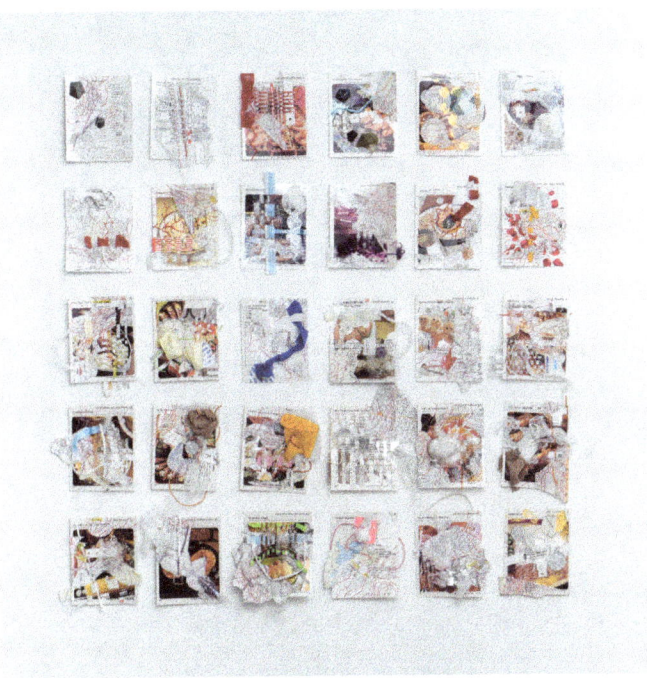

Aaron: Could you say a bit more about the images—or even icons—through which you explore ideas of healing?

Jocelyn: By its nature, my illness is invisible (as are many others'). In one sense, my work is an effort to trace the outlines of my suffering, since it has no single, monolithic cause. I am navigating around it and through it, constructing the map as I go; that is why in my work you will find maps of recognizable places torn and mismatched—it's no world that anyone knows.

So I outline it with the medical detritus that collects around me— paperwork, pill bottles, medical records, my own personal notes on my day-to-day symptoms. The gold leaf in my work is a way to sanctify those images. Turning these scraps into something beautiful is a metaphor for and a record of survival, as well as a description of the experience itself. In that sense, they're an icon of illness.

Aaron: During the periods when you felt intense, ongoing physical pain, what kinds of artwork, if any, were you able to produce?

FIGURE 31.2

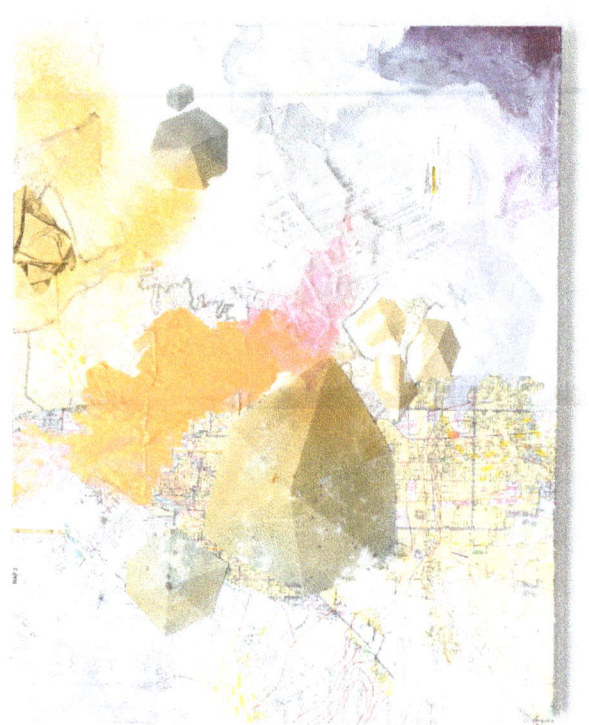

Jocelyn: Many kinds of art were possible, but I leaned on what was accessible given my physical state and my role as a caregiver.

I worked small and light, generally in two dimensions on paper, since pain makes it hard to wield heavy tools and objects. I worked out of my house using materials on hand, because it's hard to leave the place where you've shaped your environment to better care for yourself. I leaned into the photography tools I had collected for my professional work, because that documented parts of my experience for contemplation and material.

The most glaring limitation was the pace at which I could work. I planned my time so that what I hoped to accomplish in the studio would fold into my overall energy requirements for a given day. I had to break the work into very small stages; this meant I often made multiples of a single image, so I could ride a wave of energy and work on them all simultaneously with different experiments or approaches.

Aaron: Some people describe chronic pain as a sort of hermetic universe, where it's hard to think of anything else when it's going on, but also challenging to inhabit and recall when you're not in it. As you've healed, do you find yourself returning to those experiences in your work, or moving away from them?

Jocelyn: The functioning of our bodies affects what is possible for each of us in physical and temporal spaces. During active illness, the limitation that comes from the mismatch between the rest of the world and the universe of sickness increases. You think and plan around the ways you don't fit into the world.

I haven't been in remission for very long compared to how long I've been sick; my ongoing sense is one of awe and gratitude for what I'm able to do, as well as of otherworldliness. I've spent a lot of time experiencing an awakening sense of possibility, while at the same time wishing I could have felt that way during my active illness. What I know now is that the *shape* of possibility changes between the two states, but not the *number* of possibilities.

I find myself creating repeating forms. It's a way to move through the ongoing sense of grief and loss—lost time, lost ability, lost pasts, and lost potential futures. Moment by moment I repeat the grief of illness, coming to acceptance and the presence of God, and then moving to gratitude.

Aaron: You mentioned maps as a recurring theme in your work. Could you speak about why they resonate with you?

Jocelyn: I have strong early memories of maps; my father enjoyed the niche sport of orienteering and took us to orienteering meets as a family in parks and mountains around the northeastern US. Now I live in the mountains of east Tennessee—the same mountains, just farther south, and a formidable wilderness. Tenacious and resourceful peoples have made a life here for ages upon ages. I learned to navigate with a map and a compass in my youth, and here I am, in a new and somehow familiar wilderness.

Aaron: What role do you see for experimental artists in rural communities today?

Jocelyn: Experimental artists are ideally positioned to help activate a thriving culture in rural communities. Artists often see possibility and opportunity where others may not, so our role is to lead others into new ideas or ways of doing things. Artists also bring new and unexpected stories to the forefront, breaking tired stereotypes.

This is especially true for Appalachia, whose cultural representation is often less than flattering and overlooks the complex stories of the region's people. Elements of Appalachian culture are being lost because certain stereotypes have made it shameful to celebrate them. The region's artists have the ability and responsibility to share Appalachia's true stories in ways that show their beauty, strength, and ingenuity.

32. Jordan Eagles: Taking the Pulse

Jordan Eagles explores the aesthetics and ethics of blood as an artistic medium. Eagles's works are held in numerous collections including the Peabody Essex Museum, Princeton University Art Museum, University of Michigan Museum of Art and Wellcome Collection. He collaborated with the NYC Department of Health and Mental Hygiene on NYC Blood Sure and is a co-founder of Blood Equality. He lives and works in New York City.

Aaron: Do you see yourself as religious, and if so, has this self-definition influenced your work?

Jordan: I am not religious. I believe in a universal energy that is part of everything that exists, and I consider most of my work to be spiritual. I was raised in a household with art and texts from many cultures and religions. I also find spirituality in science. I am amazed that cellular details seen through a microscope can often look like telescopic images of the cosmos. The connections between body, spirit, energy, and regeneration are fundamental to my work.

Aaron: Are there any questions you find yourself struggling with over and over again?

Jordan: I would call them creative challenges. Since my practice is rooted in a few primary materials, especially blood and resin, I'm always trying to push in new directions, both conceptually and aesthetically. I'm constantly asking questions about reinvention while maintaining integrity when it comes to core materials and issues, as well as providing information and entry points for crucial policy conversations.

Aaron: Do you notice that people respond differently to your work in different settings, in a church as opposed to a gallery, say?

Jordan: Absolutely. Architecture and context can certainly affect how audiences interact with the sculptures and installations. There is a tangible history and collective consciousness that you can feel inside spiritual spaces. Blood also emits a powerful energy and has deep roots in religious iconography and myths. Both are so sacred that there is a natural synergy between the materials I use and spiritual venues.

People also often enter sacred spaces at a slower, quieter pace, with a sense of anticipatory contemplation. This can be ideal for reflecting on art and ideas. When I shared my works at Trinity Wall Street in New York City (Figure 32.1) and Guy's Chapel in London, I had unique experiences with a lot of positive feedback from the congregations.

FIGURE 32.1

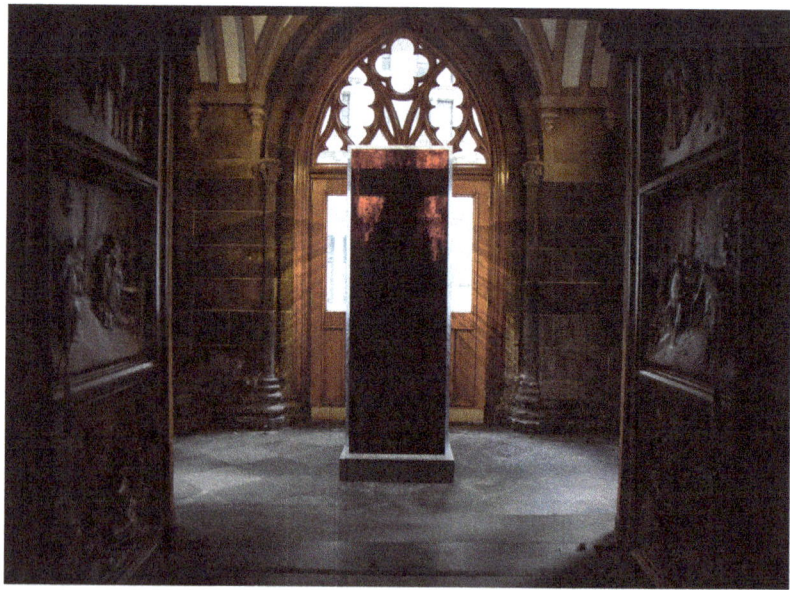

Aaron: What has been the most surprising response to your work?

Jordan: I've had many unusual responses over the years—someone almost fainted, and I've seen people cry in front of paintings. But one of the most meaningful was when a collector couple hung a large work above their bed because they wanted to conceive their first child underneath it. It was very special to me that the artwork would be associated with the creation of life in this highly personal way.

Blood can evoke a lot of emotions, and sometimes there can be a frightening association. However, because I treat blood as a life-force, with a unique method of preservation, the response I get most often is from people who are surprised how beautiful blood can be when presented in this format.

Aaron: How do you negotiate the boundary between art and activism?

Jordan: I aim to inspire conversations around equality and touch audiences beyond the art world, with the expectation that discriminatory policies can eventually be changed. The projects take the form of collaboration—which is key. Many individuals support and participate in the work, from medical supervisors to blood donors. These projects can only be accomplished through people coming together and expressing our common humanity.

Aaron: How are you thinking about your work in the midst of a pandemic?

Jordan: A lot of my work resembles cellular growth, planetary bodies, supernovas, and explosions of energy. A corona is the outermost part of the sun's atmosphere, made up of the plasma that surrounds the sun and other stars and expands millions of miles into outer space. It has been strange to look at a word—*corona*—that has so rapidly infiltrated our culture, representing disease, suffering, and death, and think about its other connotations.

In all my projects that involve human blood, I create additional sculptures out of the blood bags, collection tubes, latex gloves, protective gear, and anything that comes in contact with the blood during the art-making process—all of which is preserved in resin (Figure 32.2). The current shortage of protective gear for medical workers is reminding me of these works and making me think about how we might relate to these materials going forward.

Most importantly, as our society deals with COVID-19, I am reading about the immediate need for blood donors because of shortages due to the pandemic. This reaffirms the need for the US government to update its discriminatory blood donation policy to allow gay and bisexual men to donate blood and participate in saving lives without any deferral period based on gender or sexual orientation.

FIGURE 32.2

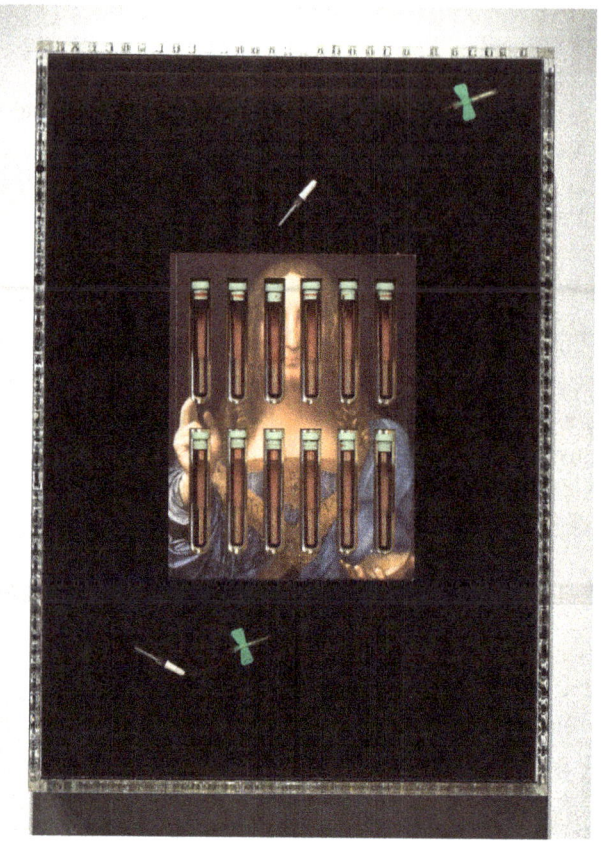

Aaron: What are your hopes for the immediate future?

Jordan: I hope we can beat this virus soon and get back to being physically close to one another again. There is nothing like experiencing art in person with friends and loved ones.

Bibliography

Ammerman, Nancy Tatom. *Sacred Stories, Spiritual Tribes: Finding Religion in Everyday Life*. Oxford: Oxford University Press, 2013.

"The Arts." *The Catholic League*, January 2015. http://www.catholicleague.org/the-arts-15/.

Auping, Michael. "Impure Thoughts: On Guston's Abstractions." In *Philip Guston Retrospective*, edited by Pam Hatley, 37–52. London: Thames & Hudson and the Royal Academy of Arts, 2003.

Bland, Kalman. *The Artless Jew: Medieval and Modern Affirmations and Denials of the Visual*. Princeton: Princeton University Press, 2000.

Boylan, Alexis. "Introduction." In *Thomas Kinkade: The Painter in the Mall*, edited by Alexis Boylan, 1–28. Durham, NC: Duke University Press, 2011.

Breslin, James. *Mark Rothko: A Biography*. Chicago: University of Chicago Press, 1993.

Bryant, Aaron. "Curator's Corner." https://imagejournal.org/article/curators-corner-national-museum-of-african-american-history-and-culture/.

Burge, Ryan P. *The Nones: Where They Came From, Who They Are, and Where They Are Going*. Minneapolis: Fortress, 2021.

"The Coexist Pilgrimage—People of Faith Walk as People of Peace." https://www.interfaith.cam.ac.uk/events/coexistpilgrimage.

Cross, William R. *Winslow Homer: American Passage*. New York: Farrar, Straus and Giroux: 2022.

Crumb, R. *Genesis*. New York: W. W. Norton, 2009.

Day, Jon. *Cyclogeography: Journeys of a London Bicycle Courier*. London: Notting Hill Editions, 2016.

De Botton, Alain. "Should Art Really Be for Its Own Sake Alone?" *The Guardian*, January 20, 2012. www.theguardian.com/commentisfree/2012/jan/20/art-museums-churches.

De Duve, Thierry. *Kant after Duchamp*. Cambridge: MIT Press, 1996.

DharmaWheels. https://dharmawheels.org/.

Dixon, John W., Jr. "The Bible in American Painting." In *The Bible and American Arts and Letters*, edited by Giles Gunn, 157–85. Philadelphia: Fortress, 1983.

Drescher, Elizabeth. *Choosing Our Religion: The Spiritual Lives of America's Nones*. New York: Oxford University Press, 2016.

Dryden, John. "*Annus Mirabilis*." In *John Dryden: Selected Poems*, edited by Steven Zwicker and David Bywaters, 26–89. London: Penguin, 2001.

Duncan, Carol. *Civilizing Rituals: Inside Public Art Museums*. London: Routledge, 1995.

Elkins, James. *Pictures and Tears: A History of People Who Have Cried in Front of Paintings.* London: Routledge, 2001.

El-Mecky, Nausikaä. "Spectacular Destruction." https://imagejournal.org/article/spectacular-destruction.

"Faith over Fear: Choosing Unity Over Extremism." Washington, DC, 2015. https://cathedral.org/wp-content/uploads/2016/04/20151220FaithoverFear.pdf.

Francis, Philip. "A Hand Outstretched in Darkness: Evangelical Encounters with Art." In *Religion and Sight,* edited by Louise Child and Aaron Rosen, 182–99. Sheffield, UK: Equinox, 2020.

Freedberg, David. *The Power of Images: Studies in the History and Theory of Response.* Chicago: University of Chicago Press, 1989.

Fry, Stephen. "Foreword." In *In League with Devils,* by Michael Petry, 3. London: MoCA, 2023.

Ginzberg, Louis. *The Legends of the Jews.* Vol. 1. Translated by Henrietta Szold. New York: Jewish Publication Society of America, 1909.

Greenberg, Clement. *Art and Culture.* Boston: Beacon, 1989.

Hayes, Christine Elizabeth. *Between the Babylonian and Palestinian Talmuds: Accounting for Halakhic Difference in Selected Sugyot from Tractate Avodah Zarah.* Oxford: Oxford University Press, 1997.

Heschel, Abraham Joshua. *God in Search of Man: A Philosophy of Judaism.* New York: Farrar, Straus and Giroux, 1976.

Icons: Worship and Adoration. Edited by Christoph Grunenberg and Eva Fischer-Hausdorf. Bremen, Germany: Hirmer/ Kunsthalle Bremen, 2019.

The Image of Christ: The Catalogue of the Exhibition Seeing Salvation. Edited by Susanna Avery-Quash and Gabriele Finaldi. London: The National Gallery, 2000.

Jones, Jonathan. "Hallelujah! Why Bill Viola's Martyrs Altarpiece at St Paul's Is to Die For." *The Guardian,* May 21, 2014.

Kennedy, Randy. "Museum of Biblical Art to Close, Despite Recent Crowds." *The New York Times,* April 28, 2015. https://www.nytimes.com/2015/04/29/arts/design/museum-of-biblical-art-to-close-despite-recent-crowds.html.

Klingelfuss Jessica. "Theaster Gates hits all the high notes in Bristol's Temple Church." *Wallpaper*,* October 30, 2015.

Knight, Christopher. "Gay Art: The Catholic League Responds to Commentary on 'Anti-Gay Bullying.'" *Los Angeles Times,* January 22, 2011. http://latimesblogs.latimes.com/culturemonster/2011/01/gay-art-the-catholic-league-responds-to-commentary-on-anti-gay-bullying-1.html.

Krauss, Rosalind. *The Originality of the Avant-Garde and Other Modernist Myths.* Cambridge: MIT Press, 1985.

In League with Devils: Michael Petry. Edited by Michael Petry. MoCA, London and The Dadian Gallery, Washington, DC: 2023.

Levi, Primo. *The Periodic Table.* Translated by Raymond Rosenthal. New York: Schocken, 1984.

Mayer, Musa. "My father, Philip Guston." *The New York Times,* August 7, 1988.

Merton, Thomas. *New Seeds of Contemplation.* New York: New Directions, 2007.

Mitchell, W. J. T. *What Do Pictures Want?* Chicago: University of Chicago Press, 2005.

Moneo, Rafael. "Architecture as a Vehicle for Religious Experience: The Los Angeles Cathedral." In *Constructing the Ineffable: Contemporary Sacred Architecture,* edited by Karla Britton, 159–69. New Haven: Yale University Press, 2010.

Morgan, David. "The Art of Jon McNaughton, the Tea Party's Painter." *Religion & Politics*, July 25, 2012. http://religionandpolitics.org/2012/07/25/the-tea-partys-painter-the-art-of-jon-mcnaughton/.

———. *The Sacred Gaze: Religious Visual Culture in Theory and Practice*. Berkeley: University of California Press, 2005.

———. *Visual Piety*. Berkeley: University of California Press, 1998.

Museum of the Bible. "Research." https://www.museumofthebible.org/research.

O'Kane, Martin. *Painting the Text: The Artist as Biblical Interpreter*. Sheffield, UK: Sheffield Phoenix, 2009.

Olin, Margaret. *The Nation without Art: Examining Modern Discourses on Jewish Art*. Lincoln: University of Nebraska Press, 2001.

Paine, Crispin. *Religious Objects in Museums: Private Lives and Public Duties*. London: Bloomsbury, 2013.

Panter, Gary. *Songy of Paradise*. Seattle: Fantagraphics, 2017.

Parker, Rosalind. "The Museum Space as a Mediator of Religious Experience: Sacred Journeys at the British Museum." In *Visualising a Sacred City: London, Art and Religion*, edited by Ben Quash, Chloë Reddaway, and Aaron Rosen, 257–72. London: I. B. Tauris, 2016.

Perl, AnnMarie. "A Belated 'Breakthrough' to Abstraction." *In Focus*: Meyron *1960–1 by Franz Kline*. London: Tate, 2017. www.tate.org.uk/research/publications/in-focus/meryon.

Pickstone, Charles. "Art's Last Icon: Malevich's *Black Square* Revisited." In *Visual Theology: Forming and Transforming the Community through the Arts*, edited by Robin Jensen and Kimberly J. Vrudny, 2–10. Collegeville, MN: Michael Glazier/Liturgical, 2009.

Pincus-Witten, Robert. "Six Propositions on Jewish Art." *Arts Magazine* 50 (1975) 66–69.

Plate, S. Brent, and Aaron Rosen. "*Stations of the Cross* Exhibition in London." *Material Religion: The Journal of Objects, Art and Belief* 12/2 (June 2016) 255–57.

Raphael, Melissa. *Judaism and the Visual Image: A Jewish Theology of Art*. London: Continuum, 2009.

Restany, Pierre. "Yves Klein e la mistica di Santa Rita da Cascia." *Editoriale Domus* (1981) 15. http://www.yvesklein.com/en/articles/view/16/the-ex-voto-to-st-rita-da-cascia.

Rilke, Rainer Maria. "Archaic Torso of Apollo." In *The Selected Poetry of Rainer Maria Rilke*, edited and translated by Stephen Mitchell, 62. New York: Vintage, 1989.

Rose, Barbara. *Monochromes: From Malevich to the Present*. Berkeley: University of California Press, 2006.

Rosen, Aaron. "Art, Heritage, and Power." In *The Bloomsbury Handbook of Religion and Heritage in Contemporary Europe*, edited by Todd Weir and Lieke Wijnia, 389–92. London: Bloomsbury, 2023.

———. *Art and Religion in the 21st Century*. London: Thames & Hudson, 2015.

———. "The Bible in American Visual Art." In *The Bible in America*, edited by Claudia Setzer and David Shefferman, 113–31. Atlanta: Society of Biblical Literature, 2020.

———. *Brushes with Faith: Reflections and Conversations on Contemporary Art*. Eugene, OR: Cascade, 2019.

———. "Exhibition as Pilgrimage: Visual Strategies for Interfaith Dialogue." In *Religion and Contemporary Art: A Curious Accord*, edited by Ron Bernier and Rachel Smith, 103–16. Routledge, 2023.

———. *Imagining Jewish Art: Encounters with the Masters in Chagall, Guston, and Kitaj*. London: Legenda, 2009.

BIBLIOGRAPHY

———. "Jewish Artists in Christian Spaces: Chagall, Rothko, and Nevelson." In *Revisiting the Rothko Chapel*, edited by Annie Cohen-Solal and Aaron Rosen, 135–54. Turnhout, Belgium: Brepols, 2025.

———. "Monochromes and Monotheisms." In *Bosco Sodi: Heavens and the Earth*, Blain/Southern Gallery, London (January 2019) 18–32.

———. "Remembering the Future in a Land of Forgotten Dreams." *Times Higher Education* (June 20, 2013).

———. "Unpacking the Bible: The Museum of Biblical Art." *Art & Christianity* 59 (Autumn 2009) n.p.

———. *What Would Jesus See? Ways of Looking at a Disorienting World*. Minneapolis: Broadleaf, 2023.

Rosen, Aaron, and Yasser Tabbaa. "Jewish and Muslim Art and Aesthetics." In *Routledge Handbook of Muslim-Jewish Relations*, edited by Josef Meri, 449–73. London: Routledge, 2016.

Ross, Steve. *Marked*. New York: Seabury, 2005.

Rowell, Margit. "Ad Reinhardt: Style as Recurrence." In *Ad Reinhardt and Color*, 11–27. New York: Guggenheim, 1980.

Rushkoff, Douglas, and Liam Sharp. *Testament: Akedah*. New York: Vertigo, 2006.

Saleem, Shahed. *The British Mosque: An Architectural and Social History*. London: Historic England, 2018.

Salkeld, Lauren, interviewing Sam Van Aken. "The Tree of 40 Fruit Is Exactly as Awesome as It Sounds." Epicurious. http://www.epicurious.com/articlesguides/chefsexperts/interviews/sam-van-aken-interview.

Schimmel, Annemarie. "Calligraphy and Islamic Culture." In *Religion, Art, and Visual Culture: A Cross-Cultural Reader*, edited by S. Brent Plate, 106–11. New York: Palgrave, 2002.

Staten, Henry. "Clement Greenberg, Radical Painting, and the Logic of Modernism." *Angelaki: Journal of the Theoretical Humanities* 7/1 (April 2002) 73–88.

Stations of the Cross. Henry Luce III Center for the Arts & Religion. www.luceartsandreligion.org/stations-of-the-cross.

Stella, Frank. "Black Painting." *The Brooklyn Rail*, Special Issue (January 16, 2014). https://brooklynrail.org/2014/01/artists-on-ad/black-painting.

Thompson, Craig. *Blankets*. Marietta, GA: Top Shelf, 2003.

———. *Habibi*. New York: Faber & Faber, 2011.

Turner, Victor, and Edith Turner. *Image and Pilgrimage in Christian Culture*. New York: Columbia University Press, 1978.

Van der Leeuw, Gerardus. *Religion in Essence and Manifestation*. Translated by J. E. Turner with appendices incorporating the additions to the second German edition by Hans H. Penner. Princeton: Princeton University Press, 1986.

Varnedoe, Kirk. *Pictures of Nothing: Abstract Art since Pollock*. Princeton: Princeton University Press, 2006.

Waldman, J. T. *Megillat Esther*. Philadelphia: Jewish Publication Society, 2005.

"Walk the Walk." https://walkthewalk2020.us/.

Weevers, Arent. *Musings about Art, Body and Spirituality: Arent Weevers Multimedia Installations 2000–2021*. Hengelo, The Netherlands, 2021.

Weil, Simone. *Gravity and Grace*. Translated by Arthur Wills. Lincoln, NE: Bison, 1997.

Wuthnow, Robert. *Creative Spirituality: The Way of the Artist*. Berkeley: University of California Press, 2001.

Zauzmer, Julie, and Sarah Pulliam Bailey. "Hobby Lobby's $3 Million Smuggling Case Casts a Cloud over the Museum of the Bible." *The Washington Post*, July 6, 2017. https://www.washingtonpost.com/news/acts-of-faith/wp/2017/07/06/hobby-lobbys-3-million-smuggling-case-casts-a-cloud-over-the-museum-of-the-bible/?utm_term=.448b24746964.

www.ingramcontent.com/pod-product-compliance
Lightning Source LLC
Chambersburg PA
CBHW070540220526
45467CB00003B/1007